COACHING PEOPLE WITH
ASPERGER'S SYNDROME

COACHING PEOPLE WITH ASPERGER'S SYNDROME

Bill Goodyear

KARNAC

First published in 2008 by
Karnac Books Ltd
118 Finchley Road
London NW3 5HT

British Library Cataloguing in Publication Data

A C.I.P. for this book is available from the British Library

ISBN13: 978–1–85575–413–3

Edited, designed, and produced by
Florence Production Ltd, Stoodleigh, Devon
www.florenceproduction.co.uk

www.karnacbooks.com

CONTENTS

ACKNOWLEDGEMENTS

A fter 60 years, there are so many people who have made a contribution to my learning and development. Ian McDermott taught me Neuro Linguistic Programming in a sublime and subtle way. Over the years later I still have his voice in my head! Maggie Rigg gave me my first job in Autism, changing the course of my life for ever. Celia and I developed a joint love of this curious work as we raised our children, and she still challenges me to be even more curious, and Patrice and Luly at the Paris Play-ground are introducing me to a whole new way of understanding co-active coaching. While I owe my gratitude to these good people, it is, of course, the families and the people with Asperger's who have allowed me to get close enough to them who have really made the great contribution—Andrew, Prem, Josh, Stefan, and many many others—Mark, Dan, Nicky, David from the old school, amongst many others and, of course, Robyn. Thank you all.

ABOUT THE AUTHOR

Bill has spent a lifetime amongst people with autism, first as a teacher in one of the first schools founded by the National Autistic Society, then in a local voluntary society to his own school, offering education to a group of children who were excluded from any education at the time, and in his Asperger Coaching practice which he has been operating for nearly 20 years. In that time he has met hundreds of families living with autism and Asperger's syndrome and attended endless conferences exploring new research.

He is father of three exciting and grown up children, a keen photographer and an unstoppable guitar player, and while he is a good cook, he is lousy at gardening.

Having lived in Folkestone, Ealing, Andover, Adlestrop, Peterborough and Rotherham, he currently lives in London and travels around talking about Asperger's syndrome, autism and life, and is developing his coaching into the neuro typical world, especially focussing on supporting people in making their own creative projects happen.

He mainly uses his lifetime's experience of autism spectrum disorders to support families living with Asperger's, and within that he is finding ways to help mainstream organisations include people with Asperger and to help those with Asperger's to be included.

PREFACE

I spend more time in the company of people with Asperger's than I do with neurotypicals.[1] I have been coaching them for nearly twenty years now, and have met hundreds of families, children and adults who are all living with Asperger's syndrome. Of course I have not met those who are successfully living with the condition. Indeed, many of those people may not even realise why it is that they all too often feel a bit dissatisfied or confused about their social lives, why they didn't quite get that promotion, or laugh at that joke.

I have visited doctors' surgeries, dentists, psychiatric wards and prisons in my work, been in places where I really didn't want the tea I was offered, and been in others where I really did need a drink but was not offered anything. I have witnessed violence, learnt about medication and attended endless meetings in which people seemed to be finding ways to avoid admitting that they could not help. I have listened to people cry their hearts out because they are so upset about the treatment their son or daughter is receiving, and I have been party to many long phone calls which tried to get that

---

1. Neurotypical (NT) is a term that describes those of us who do not have neurodiversity, i.e. the majority population.

situation changed. I have helped young men move out of their family home and into their flats, and I have shared my cooking skills. Most of my time has gone on long conversations which eventually come round to that old question: "What do you want?"—rapidly followed by "And how will you go about getting it?"

Although it is really difficult to find a model of the condition— "Oh that's what people with Asperger's are like!"—I can say that most of the people I have got to know are good people; often they are frustrated and sometimes not in control of their anger, but these are few compared to the many who are trying to find a way to make the world work for them so they don't feel excluded. I have used real experiences to illustrate my writing (names are all changed of course), so that you can meet some of the people I have met in my time.

Sixty years after it was first identified, Asperger's syndrome is still not fully understood scientifically, medically, socially or psychologically. It is a developmental disorder (affecting your experience as you grow up), and in my view a lot of the commonly found negative thinking patterns are learnt. In fact the root cause of the condition is probably only to do with your perception—and perhaps your digestion.

I wrote this book because I want to offer a cohesive view of how people with this condition go about their lives and what can be done to help them. Although coaching is essentially a dialogue between two people, it is fuelled by some deep understandings and ways of thinking that allow the coach to build a beneficial influence, although of course it is the subjects of the coaching who have to do all the hard work and make the changes in the way they experience their lives.

There is very little support available in the UK, and what there is tends to be either medication or short interventions. Most of the rest is about mopping up after the crisis, and is often not specifically designed or therapeutic. People spend long hours in waiting rooms and on waiting lists in the hope that someone can help, and are frequently disappointed. This book is about a can-do solution which I want to share more widely.

In this book, I will be exploring how people affected by the condition—or perhaps conditions—known as Asperger's syndrome can best be supported in living successfully with it. This will involve going into how the condition arises, the best understanding of the condition that is currently available, summarising the knowledge coming out of research, and considering how the condition actually affects individuals. Throughout I will be referring to real people I have met. Over more than 35 years in the autism business I have met hundreds of individuals in their families, and I have worked closely with many of them in coaching and teaching situations. I have also worked closely with their families in the course of this exploration, and these experiences of individual stories will be used to counterbalance the generalities that necessarily arise when one examines research and theory, which is constantly trying to identify similarities in order to create a useful pattern.

I am not propounding a miracle cure, or even a solution that will work for everyone in this group, but I am suggesting that a new, accessible, though perhaps slightly quirky approach can make a significant difference to some, and that wider application is worth exploring.

Also, of course, we can take a look at what would help and contrast this to what actually exists in terms of useful and accessible services: I have my opinions, though I am very willing to be contra-dicted—it is never possible to be up to date with all developments. However, the group is disparate, and services, in my experience, seem to find it hard to reach the whole waveband within the spectrum.

My experience tells me that a whole area of this developmental disorder has been somewhat marginalized by the pathological approach deriving from the scientific reductionist approach which has led the development of understanding and support for these people. This area, developmental disorder, is one which is shared between people with Asperger's and the neurotypical population, and for which there is a present-day explosion of understanding and technique. My recent experience has derived from exploring how this new technology of personal change can be directed at this population so they can feel happy and confident enough to make the most of their abilities.

Lastly, I will explore how the family is central to the process of supporting their children with Asperger's in achieving real and full independence without falling prey to the many real risks that exist, and consider briefly how coaching avoids some of the traps present services fall into. Beyond this there is a sprinkling of coaching tips and stories to make the text more relevant and interesting, as well as some ideas about specific and "hot" topics.

I have written this in quite a personal way, and have freely used the first person. This is because most of what I write in fact arises out of my own experience. I must make the usual comment here that whilst I have drawn freely on the presentations and conversations of many, most of them more learned than me, I accept all the responsibility for the resulting work which you now hold in your hands—most of the information here is the result of the work of others, and any mistakes, omissions and misinterpretations are mine.

A note about terminology. When I have to, I identify the person with Asperger's as male (ten men are affected to every woman), though I have met several women who are on the spectrum, and I apologise to them and their sisters. There are, by the way, suggestions from Tony Attwood and Simon Baron-Cohen that the differential between the sexes may not be so great, but that women are either differently affected or learn to cope better and hence are less frequently diagnosed. Also, I sometimes refer to the group as Aspies and to the rest of us as NTs. It seems to me that Aspie is a friendly term created or accepted from within the community, and NT seems a satisfactorily jargony way to deal with the rest of us neurotypicals, as we are known.

Many people with Asperger's in particular, and autism in general, have overlapping conditions (they might also have schizophrenia or dyslexia, for instance). These are known as co-morbid conditions.

Where I talk about autism, I am usually referring to the whole spectrum, including Asperger's. Where I refer to Asperger's syndrome, of course, I am referring to that condition specifically. Of course the phrase "the spectrum" indicates the entirety of autistic disorders—people are often described as "on the spectrum".

INTRODUCTION

Annie is 20 years old. She is a student, just about to go to university on an IT course. She was born prematurely, staggered though primary school as an autistic child, went to a small rural secondary school, was predictably bullied and locked in the toilets, and was ostracised in her village. She has hemiplegia, an inability to recognise faces (she refers to people's shoes instead—she is short), dyslexia, dyscalculia and a range of other specific conditions. She bangs her head and bites her arm when she is bored, and is hypersensitive to a range of sensory information— smells, loud noises, bright lights, certain touch sensations. She has developed a business as a trainer explaining Asperger's syndrome, and is getting enough work to justify her hoping to pay her way through university without using a student loan. Her feedback sheets are better than mine and her hourly rate is higher than mine. She has a few friends, but has just completed a two-year course without making social contact with any of her peers. When she gets anxious, her conversation returns to a few repeated themes. She likes Pink Floyd and knows everything about them, and has just been accepted as a mentor of children with Asperger's.

Back in 1944, Hans Asperger, an Austrian psychiatrist, first identified this condition, and along with other autistic spectrum disorders it has been subject to a great deal of medical and scientific research over the subsequent half century, which has massively improved our understanding of how it arises and what causes it. Educationalists and psychologists have added to our knowledge in terms of what helps these people to develop a satisfactory life, though Asperger's Syndrome remains a condition which is poorly understood and poorly recognised, and for which there is very little specific support.

Medical science reduces things to their constituent parts and focuses on the problems, finding it more difficult to join disparate pieces of knowledge and understanding together. Although this has been useful, the treatments which have arisen from this way of thought tend to be aimed at the constituent conditions (the bits that make up the problem, such as obsessive or compulsive behaviour, anxiety etc) or the co-morbid conditions (the conditions that exist alongside it, such as schizophrenia, cerebral palsy, colour-blindness etc). What I notice is that the fruits of this scientific process are reflected in how we work with Asperger's, in that a lot of attention is directed at helping people to manage or overcome the problem, or at setting up services which can tolerate this behaviour. There has been less focus on finding ways to help people live successfully and independently with this condition.

Current support is apparently often inappropriate and inaccessible, and though people with Asperger's syndrome have undoubted abilities, they often experience difficulties in their lives that prevent them from using these abilities. This seems to be true beyond the shores of the UK—parents in the USA and Australia report similar experiences, and although we do know that some people with Asperger's syndrome have achieved fame and fortune, it seems that whilst we can expect achievers, we can also expect underachievers. Of course there are also significant numbers of people who are so affected by the condition that they do need long-term support or even care.

There are vast areas of similarity between people with Asperger's syndrome and neurotypicals (those of us whose nervous system is typical and who therefore do not suffer from Asperger's, autism, dyspraxia, Tourette's, etc): on a genetic level the similarities between us are profound. It seems fair to assume, therefore, that what helps us will also help them. We are certainly similar in that bad experiences lead to us developing bad psychology. People, both neurotypical and Asperger's, sometimes have real reasons to be frightened, depressed, unwilling to try, dreamy, isolated, off on their own. This is not a product of their Asperger's but of their experience, just like the rest of us.

However, the good news is that there are ways to remediate negative thinking, some of which are only just being recognised. Many disciplines now try to find routes towards positive states of mind rather than routes away from negative ones, and this journey is, in my view, the key to supporting people with Asperger's in living a successful life.

However, unless things go extraordinarily well, families are left holding the baby, and as the child grows into adult life they have to go against the grain of the natural response. Especially in adult life, but also in preparation for the youngster moving away from adolescence, coaching the family is a stronger move than focusing solely on the individual. Of course, life expectancy tells us that these people have to make their own choices in the end, as they will outlive their parents. So every adult needs to develop a level of autonomy; but for most people with Asperger's syndrome it is also true that their families need to know that progress does not involve unacceptable risk.

This book is about my experiences and thinking developed in years of coaching people with Asperger's syndrome. Coaching is a solution that brings people closer into the mainstream: unlike current services, coaching is accessible, flexible, and affordable. It also offers some aspects that most support currently misses, and so it can in some ways be considered to be somewhat of a "barefoot" approach.

I hope I have written a very practical book, although much of it is focused on understanding the condition and the remedy: because coaching is such an ephemeral art and Asperger's is a confusing condition, it is important to understand the underlying thinking behind an apparently gentle and easy approach. Much of the problem in Asperger's arises out of experience and is learned in childhood and adult life. Accepting this opens the door to the application of a range of approaches used in mainstream life, but also focuses attention on the core nature of the problem itself, which is a hard nut to crack: everyone with Asperger's I have met (and I have met many) is as different one from the other as all the mainstream neurotypical people I have met. There are patterns, of course, but these guys are shy and the patterns have to be sought out. Sometimes it just seems as though each person is an individual with nothing in common, and this makes life much more difficult—Asperger's is an invisible disability.

So although this is (I hope) a thoughtful book which is full of theories and reflection, it is also littered with Coaching Tips. So as not to interrupt the flow of reading too badly, they appear in brief in the text and are expanded upon at the end. I have also illuminated my writing with stories from real life. No doubt some people will recognise themselves, though the names and circumstances are all changed to protect everyone's identity. I want to thank them all, as well as their families, for sharing their stories with me. For a long time now I have been talking to more people with Asperger's in a week than with neurotypicals—nice people! I wish I had been able to help more of them in a more complete way, but the cards are still stacked against you if you are living with this condition. It has always been hard to find the necessary cash to fund long-term intensive work, and the problems, if unchecked, become more profound over the years, of course, and harder to undo. On top of this are my own imperfections in doing the work, which should not be under-estimated. Always enthusiastic (or almost!) and often over-ready to have a go, I feel as though I have invented a work discipline, trodden on a few toes on the way and disappointed many (for which I can only apologise), but hope I have helped a few.

PART I

ALL ABOUT ASPERGER'S
SYNDROME

INTRODUCTION

This book is split into three parts. This part is about the condition of Asperger's syndrome, discussing in detail what it is, how it arises and how it manifests itself. I have also taken the time to discuss the possibilities of progress and the need for support.

In all I have written, I have mixed research that I have come across in the course of my life: at conferences and seminars, though the Internet and in books, and have compared that with direct experience—my own and that of the many people I have met and talked with over the years. To an extent I suppose I have developed my own theories, or at least enriched the map of the knowledge we currently enjoy, mixing that with the reality I meet and my understanding of how people function and progress.

CHAPTER ONE

Asperger's syndrome—overview

Ravi is 34. He lives in a flat designed for people recovering from mental ill health, having been diagnosed as schizophrenic and treated accordingly in his teens. He was diagnosed as having Asperger's syndrome about four years ago. After 15 years he is reducing his medication, and will be off it all in a year if all goes well. He has moved past being angry and violent with his family, and has spent several years wandering around shopping centres fantasising. He is now at college preparing for an access to higher education course in order to qualify for university. He has learnt to manage his fear of being looked at, and is now learning to manage his time and to read for study. He is quiet, polite and passive, and is hoping to get a girlfriend soon. He is beginning to speak out in groups and is considering joining an acting class for fun.

I qualified as a teacher after a few years in which I realised I was going to work with children in one form or another: I was first introduced to mentally handicapped children and adults (as they were then known) in my early twenties. I then went to work with maladjusted children for a brief while, then to an adventure playground where we accepted all comers—the neurotypicals of the future. Awakening slowly, I then went off to train as a teacher and earned a degree in education. The first (and last!) teaching job I ever held was as a teacher of autistic children, which I took on in 1981, working for the National Autistic Society only 16 years after the first ever school for autistic children had been opened. I became principal of the school some time later, then moved into the world of adult provision (a total mystery for teachers at that time), thence to management consultant (a total mystery for all of us to this day), then to training, and finally to the adventure of developing a business coaching adults with Asperger's syndrome, which I began in total frustration about 17 years ago—better to do something than keep on complaining that no-one does anything. So I started a business uniquely offering coaching to people with Asperger's syndrome, which I have been doing ever since, sometimes employing others to support me.

So here is my argument in brief: Asperger's syndrome hinders Aspies in understanding others, communicating effectively, and thinking flexibly. Because of this, they have difficult lives and are isolated in an intensely social world. There has been a weight of work done on how this population is different from the mainstream neurotypical population. Whilst not dismissing this in any way, I am suggesting that we should also focus on the similarities, so that we can adapt existing techniques to support these people in living successfully with this condition.

Autism is still a mystery at its roots: currently, the best assumption is that in the first place there is some genetic difference. If this arises through inheritance, then the nature-nurture debate becomes interesting because it will bring attention to questioning how much of the defining behaviour is learnt within the family and how much derives from deviance in the physiological blueprint and consequent impaired or unusual perception mechanisms. Alternatively, it may derive from first-generation adaptation or damage. There may be other causes too: these things are not clarified yet, and the research continues. It seems that the best guess at this stage is that there is a strong likelihood that there is a genetic component to the conditions which give rise to autism and Asperger's syndrome. Other causes may also exist, and there may be an interaction of several overlapping separate causes. Indeed, it may be a confluence of two or more separate conditions creating the Triad of Impairments which we call autism, any of which could exist separately in others. It also seems likely that an environmental insult can trigger a predisposition and generate circumstances in which autism develops. So the first level of difference is likely to be identified as a genetic predisposition, with some levels of the condition being perhaps triggered by an event, often (but not always) pre- or perinatal. However, there is now a recognition that the condition can emerge later in life, perhaps at 3 or 4 years old, so it may be that this predisposition can be triggered at that comparatively late stage in life. It may also be that Asperger's syndrome, and possibly autism, can arise spontaneously, with no inherited factors leading the process.

> Michael was perfectly normal, according to his parents, until his fourth birthday party. He invited his friends, and then when they all arrived, he "vanished upstairs, stayed in his bedroom throughout and came down autistic". He lost his speech and became very nervous, and developed Asperger's syndrome to the point where he needed specialist education. I can only think that he lost his confidence so much, and was so frightened by this experience of hearing all his friends having a good time but feeling unable to join in, that he experienced a collapse of confidence which triggered his condition.

In all events, it seems that the genetic difference gives rise to a number of systemic differences within the person, possibly beginning with the architecture of the brain and nervous system. Again, these are not fully described, categorised or understood yet, although one strong underlying feature seems to be a specific difference in the way people with autism perceive sensation. It may be that they are particularly sensitive to some or all of sound, touch, light, smell and taste. In other cases it may be that they are indifferent to any of these sensory inputs. This may be to do with the way this incoming data is processed, or it may be that the initial perception is unusual in some way. Throughout life, it is certainly clear that responses to the environment can be major causes of stress in children and adults on the spectrum, slowing down their ability to make sense of the world.

The condition apparently arises from brain structure and consequent function, and is diagnosed by observing behaviour and considering the life story: what the person did and now does creates the symptoms that serve as diagnostic indicators. These behaviours, enshrined in DSM IV, ICD 10 and other places, have all been taken from real observation, and are considered to be evidence for the presence of the Triad of Impairments. This relatively new formulation, created by Lorna Wing and Judith Gould in 1979, has helped our understanding no end. The shape of the whole condition of autism has been understood in more detail as research continues, and the parameters have shifted to the point where we now talk of the "autistic spectrum disorders" in order to include the varieties more evenly.

Medical science, however, tends to focus on what is wrong, and dissects problems in order to understand the constituent parts. This approach, whilst necessary and valuable, and one of the foremost drivers in human progress, has its drawbacks for this population. Current medical treatment tends to look for those who are falling into a crisis of one sort or another, for instance depression, anxiety, paranoia, fantasy and rage. Treatments focus on these parts of the personality's function, avoiding the interaction within the personality that arises from this condition. Support services tend to offer residential or perhaps day support to those who cannot manage independently, though naturally there are always exceptions. Perhaps more work needs to be done to explore how people can be supported in developing successful lives before things go so wrong.

Now, if you are born with Asperger's, you slowly move though life discovering how everyone else knows what to do and does it without bothering about you, except for occasionally laughing at you and probably bullying you in your teenage years, or at least sometimes getting angry with you for unspecified reasons. You would be lucky to escape this: if you do, then you are unusual, though you may well be doing your best to keep your head down, learning that the rest of the world does indeed go on without you whilst you occupy yourself with some interesting and satisfying alternative. Probably there are people with Asperger tendencies who have satisfying lives without ever being diagnosed or noticed as being pathological, but of course it is hard to find them. Those we do find are the ones who are having some significant difficulty with their lives; in fact, life can be a succession of difficult experiences for them. All we know is that early intervention will help enormously. I am suggesting that we can go further than we usually do in ensuring that this intervention is designed to support the development of positive attitudes and beliefs. For those who have been through the mill it may be too late, but my experience is that at least some will be able to get a hold of their life and overcome past negative experiences.

In addition to the Triad of Impairments (difficulty with communication, relationships and rigidity of thought), many people with Asperger's have sensory sensitivities. These can be pervasive and extremely uncomfortable to deal with. Hypersensitivity can distract attention from the job in hand, so kitchen smells in the classroom, for instance, can take your concentration away. Sudden noises can induce instant panic and confusion, so fire bell testing can wreck a morning in school or college. Imagine a busy train station or airport: crowds of noisy, ill-disciplined NTs, some with squawking children, others shouting into their mobile phones, every trolley with squeaky wheels, hard-to-hear PA announcements coming out at alarmingly frequent intervals in poorly pronounced and distorted PA-speak. People bang into you, let alone invade your personal space. The monitor lights flicker and are illuminated by the sun, so are very hard to read, and your departure time is closing in. You walk past McDonalds (or worse), and the smell makes you want to run. Where is the toilet, and how can you get there, and will it have those noisy hand driers?

James is a bright and active four-year-old. He is thrown into a tantrum by the sound of a bell, so visitors have to be warned not to ring the doorbell, and telephone conversations can be interrupted by his screaming. Alarm clocks are impossible.

How does this condition arise? Assuming that the condition is genetic, I would like to note in passing how similar Aspies are to NTs. It almost does not need saying; except that their perception is often that they are hopelessly out of step with the rest of us (Temple Grandin described herself as an "Anthropologist on Mars"—two major steps of difference). They are usually in step in terms of their ambitions: job, love, money—the usual. They are usually in step in that their mood goes up and down a bit, they get bored, or depressed by lack of structure, and they tend to take it out on those around them. Their hearts beat the same and their livers all do the same work as for the rest of us. However, these people are marginalized for being different by their peers and by society, and their subjective experience is that they are out of step in a very central way. To us it may seem less significant, but then we would say that, wouldn't we? If you had lived their life, how would you be different?

People with Asperger's syndrome may be capable of much more than they typically achieve: we know that feeling bad about yourself and feeling anxious reduces performance, so if you learnt to feel better, performance would improve. Yet we also know that Gary Numan (singer), Vernon Smith (Nobel laureate) and Satoshi Tajiri (creator of Pokémon) are in the group, and we suspect that Einstein, Newton, Jeremy Bentham, Wittgenstein and Glenn Gould, amongst others, might also have been diagnosable. Creativity is a strong strand of the Aspie experience.

Another systemic difference likely to exist in someone with this condition is a difference in their autonomic nervous system, which may be much more (or less) sensitive than is usual. In extremis, the autonomic nervous system creates the "fight or flight" reaction, in which the body adapts very rapidly and comprehensively to a perceived threat, contracting capillaries, focusing eyesight, sharpening hearing, raising the heartbeat and so on, so that the person can either run away very efficiently or is physiologically prepared to stand and fight. This is created in part by an injection of adrenaline into the blood. Interestingly, it takes hours to wash the blood clean if the energy is not used in fighting or fleeing, and men take longer over this task than women, autistic or not. Autistic people, with their over- or under-reactive system may be living with adrenaline levels that make concentration and learning very difficult.

Gene research is a new science, and we have seen the explosion in knowledge that has resulted from the sequencing of the genomes over the past few years. In 1991 Jared Diamond, physiologist and ecologist, noted that DNA in humans and chimpanzees is so similar that we could be called the third chimpanzee. Now Morris Goodman from the Wayne State University in Detroit supports this in noting that a 99.4% similarity exists in the most critical DNA sites in chimps and ourselves. With this level of congruity, he suggests that chimps should be considered as human. I mean no disrespect to chimps or to us, or to people with Asperger's; I am using this research to highlight the similarities between Aspies and ourselves. If chimps are in the same family as me, then Aspies are hardly different at all, and yet they experience the world in a very different way (and vice versa), and it is this experience that damages them so much: they learn to be different because they are excluded, which magnifies the original condition.

In terms of cognitive function and learning there are significant differences, but in terms of learning about life there is no significant difference between Aspies and NTs. In both cases, bad experiences lead to bad psychology. Aspies have many real reasons to be frightened, depressed, unwilling to try, dreamy, isolated, off on their own, and these reasons are to be found directly in their experience of life so far and their fears about what might be coming next. They learn negative thinking in response to repeated negative experiences, as we all do—though I don't know so much about the chimps! Although, as I said, I am not propounding a cure or a revolution, I am suggesting that this negative thinking, which is a surface characteristic arising from the central problem, can be attacked, and that earlier experiences could be better managed in order to avoid a lot of this pain in the first place. Happier people perform better, whether or not they have Asperger's syndrome.

Of course, the extreme flight or fight reaction represents an extreme experience, though most of us have experienced it in our lives. People with autistic spectrum disorders are less likely to have this automatic response fully under control. In fact this is part of a system within all of us which conducts a continual chemical and electrical conversation of great complexity, regulating our heartbeat, breathing, digestion and other essential life support systems. In part this is achieved through a system of interactions directed by the production and reception of the 100-plus peptides which run in our circulation system and which seem to define emotion and subjective experience.

Some of these peptides are neurotransmitters such as serotonin, and there is an established (though not conclusive) link between abnormal levels of serotonin and autism. Many other peptides appear to communicate between essential organs, the presence of one creating an adjustment in the level of another, and the resulting and continually changing cocktail of peptides in the blood relates to emotion, which directs the subjective experience of how we feel and so affects our perception of what we notice. So it seems that this condition, originating from genetic difference and difference in neurological structure and function, is also rooted in systemic physiological differences. Candace Pert's book *Molecules of Emotion* offers a wealth of information about this, though she was not directly concerned with Asperger's or autism in her work.

The child develops with slightly different brain architecture, different neurological functions in some areas, probably focusing on perception and the processing of some areas of information. Also, his emotional mechanism may well be out of alignment, and in some cases he may not be digesting the necessary nutrients from his food. All of this means that his minute-to-minute experiences may well be different to those of the neurotypical population. For instance, he may experience confusion, fear or intense interest at moments when others experience more commonplace emotions, and these differences may well create strain in relationships.

So the experience of developing with these differences in your body creates experiences that tend to lead to the development of some idiosyncratic beliefs, and whilst these are strong in most people with autism, they are particularly noticeable in people with Asperger's, as their closeness to the neurotypical group highlights the impact of different belief structures. This is worth exploring in more depth, not least because beliefs are only constructs of the mind, and so are subject to change. However, at any one time they are strong: people fight and die for their beliefs, so they are clearly significant in directing behaviour. Everyone carries around their own belief structure. I call it a structure because it seems that we create and adopt a whole set of beliefs which enable us to make sense of our experience, and that they interlock in a way that creates a kind of structure in which we live. This means that people are resistant to belief change, as one small change can threaten the whole structure. However, over time it is clear that beliefs change naturally (think about your political convictions over the last thirty years, or the time you choose to go to bed and get up now, compared with when you were a teenager).

There are ways to remediate negative thinking that are only just being recognised: for instance Positive Psychology is a discipline which has only arisen in the past five years, though it grew from the humanist psychology of Carl Rogers, Erich Fromm and Abraham Maslow. It studies how happiness and good feelings arise, focusing on how we create positive feelings rather than the more usual clinical approach of how we cure mental ill health. Neuro-Linguistic Programming (NLP) has been around for about thirty years, and attempts to understand and describe the subjective side of experience so that others can replicate desirable experiences. Beyond that, in the wider world there is an explosion of interest that started in the sixties with the New Age and focuses on "feelgood". Positive psychology is currently Harvard's largest course. Of course a study of how happiness, contentment or peacefulness arises in a mind is as valid as a study of fear, aggression or depression.

To get a feel of the contrast in focus between new psychology and old, go to a bookshop and look over the shelves. Note how much weight there is on the pathology in psychology: studies of what's wrong have led psychology for the past hundred years. It is my contention that studies of what's right might help people with Asperger's in significant ways. I will be going into this in depth later in this book. For now I just want to note that in my experience these techniques do exist and can be delivered.

I find that I am now led to focus not so much on coaching the individual but on coaching the whole family. I have come to the conclusion recently that it is a better use of my effort to coach a family than it is to work directly and solely with the person who has Asperger's. Partially this arises from my realisation that in all cases, until things go so well that the person has achieved complete and real independence, the family is left holding the baby. Services cannot be relied upon, and some people with Asperger's just do not find a way to leave the nest.

In these circumstances, parents do what they can. The natural reaction is to keep a parental overview of your child's life in which privacy and boundaries are left in a childish state rather than amended to allow for adulthood. Usually the child goes though the mill as an adolescent. Many people with Asperger's do not success-fully make this transition, and the family can become a force that supports dependence. In extremis, this can become co-dependence, in which the entire family lives by and for the problems.

To help a young person move through the process of claiming his or her rights goes right against the grain of the natural parental response, so I conclude that coaching a family to adjust its beliefs and expectations together is often a more powerful tool than coaching the individual alone, as it will help the family move to a place where it will naturally support and maintain the new-found independence that I hope results from the work I do.

Ultimately, of course, the natural laws of life expectancy tell us that the child will be all alone in later years unless siblings are co-opted, and so the work has to be designed so that the child with Asperger's moves to a point where he rules his life wisely, and this is respected because all around him know that he is safe and can be trusted not to damage himself or others. However, issues of an acceptable lifestyle may well also need to be negotiated as family members come to terms with the reality of the choices made.

I am suggesting a somewhat "barefoot doctor" approach. Current services are often inappropriate or inaccessible. Medication, education, even institutionalisation all have their place sometimes, but cost, inflexibility, waiting times arising from poor supply and heavy demand, poorly equipped staff who really do not understand, and the centralisation of services all work against the population; and of course some Government money would be helpful in developing services. The benefits gained by any of these interventions (even education) tend to decay over time if not continually supported. The barefoot approach of coaching, in contrast, is individual, accessible and flexible. It is designed to meet the needs of these unclubbable people and their families, who are themselves often disadvantaged in terms of earning ability and energy. It is accessible to anyone who has a phone, though Internet access helps. The first precept of coaching is that the coach is there to help the client explore his or her own best way forward. All families are individual and do not like prescriptive solutions, so coaching is designed specifically around the needs and aspirations of the family and the problems it faces in supporting the child into an independent and safe lifestyle; it is as flexible as necessary. It is also relatively affordable and does not necessarily rely on the intervention (sadly rarely forthcoming) of a statutory support body. Also, change within a family will support itself and is therefore very likely to be resilient over time.

Sean has just emerged from psychiatric hospital, having attempted suicide because of a number of unwelcome secrets being made available to his family after a prolonged period of blackmail. His discharge from hospital has resulted in a preliminary diagnosis being made, and he is now waiting to meet the experts at Elliot House, a National Autistic Society diagnostic centre. He has worked all his life in banking, and although the blackmailing has left him without any reserves, he can pay me to start coaching him in developing his life and understanding the condition and how it affects him.

CHAPTER TWO

What is Asperger's and why is it a problem?

Bernard is in his early forties. He lives alone with his mother, who does almost all of the domestic work, despite her heart condition. He is trained as a bookkeeper, but does not undertake any work except on a voluntary basis for a charity of which he is board member. Because his doctor lives on one side of a border and his address is on the other, he has been overlooked and ignored more than is right. Every now and then he gets a bee in his bonnet and tries to find out why people are not following clear procedure, and this creates stress for his mother. He does not know if he will retain residence of the council flat they share when his mother dies.

Asperger's syndrome is a social and communication disorder which hinders people in understanding others, communi-cating effectively, and thinking flexibly, so they have difficult lives, isolated in an intensely social world. Some create an inde-pendent life, others fall into needing institutional care, and there is a continuum of development between these two extremes. It is an autistic spectrum disorder arising from brain structure and function, and shows itself through behaviour. It is defined as a syndrome, which means that it is recognised through the close observation of behaviour and history, which in turn means that diagnosis is a skilled and imprecise art.

Research is always developing—new information is coming to us all the time. Asperger's syndrome (and autism in general) is a complex developmental disorder: initial differences in the structure and function of the brain give rise to difficulties in perception and cognition which affect the development of the child, creating additional difficulties. We know that Asperger's is a branch of autism, and as such it is defined by the Triad of Impairments: difficulties in (i) social relationships and (ii) communication, and (iii) a rigidity of thinking patterns. Asperger's in addition has a normal or high IQ score and normal syntactical language. What this means is that people affected have difficulty in facing the social world. Often they do not understand, sometimes they seem not to value usual behaviour, and sometimes they find it actively difficult or unpleasant to participate.

Tip No 1: Tell them what is required
Explain in advance, in detail and in Technicolor

Tip No 2: Set up escape routes from social situations
If a person knows he can get away if it all gets too hard, he will be stronger

In terms of communication, they may find it hard to talk unless they feel very comfortable with the other person. They may find telephone or Internet chat rooms preferable. If and when they do talk, whilst their syntax is good, they may make big and unpredictable jumps in their logic in the conversation, and may not respond well to the conversational flow. They may be more adept at speaking than at listening, and may have odd verbal habits. Additionally, of course, their body language and facial expression may be noticeably odd.

Tip No 3: Listen to the end of a speech before interrupting
It is empowering to be heard in full

Tip No 4: Ask for explanation of obtuse connections
Discover their logic before you decide there is no logic

Tip No 5: Create rapport
*Do what they are doing—let them lead, and follow
so they can feel comfortable*

Tip No 6: Check that they are understanding
*It is always good to check and go over what has
been said—never assume*

The rigidity of thought is often, though not always, a product of stress and anxiety. Aspies tend to like routines and not see the point of doing things differently. Some may have odd habits; many have special interests that consume them. Changing routine is difficult for them.

Tip No 7: Plan ahead and share the plans to allow for routines
*They may well be able to tell you what they find hard,
and you may well be able to make an escape or
avoidance plan*

As ever, when I am describing this condition, it seems that the parts of the list do not make up the whole of the condition. Children with this condition may be noticeably odd, poor sleepers, difficult or demanding, and may be solitary and restricted in their activities in comparison to what you might expect. In the teenage years the gulf shows itself, and friends may be in short supply. Bullying is so common that it should be a diagnostic point: the person with Asperger's is almost always the one who is bullied.

Tip No 8: Prevent bullying at all costs
*Bullying happens, and it damages people for the rest of their lives—
do whatever it takes to prevent it from happening rather than
trying to patch things up after the event*

Tip No 9: Empathy

Imagine what it would be like to stand in their shoes for a moment, with their fears and frustrations; let yourself feel it

In later adolescence, exam pressure sometimes gets too much and the social and academic pressure leads the child to drop out of school prematurely, though often too late for the Education Department to do anything about it. Some, however, sail through the academic and manage the social, and find their way to university. Some of those fail to make it through to the third year, torpedoed by the lack of structure. Some of those who do successfully exit the education system without a breakdown then fail to get their adult life into gear, and withdraw into the family home and their bedrooms within. Many of these then experience a breakdown of self-confidence and succumb to paranoia, depression or anxiety. Some find work; some of these lose their jobs very fast. Those who manage some security of tenure tend to underachieve and become stuck in a job that may be below their abilities.

Tip No 10: Seek continuous knowledgeable support

Everyone has a contribution to make, and the bit you do not want to hear may be the most useful

Tip No 11: Claim what you want to the point of unreasonableness: do not accept No

Whether with the person who has Asperger's or with professionals or with your partner, you have a right to be heard and understood, and those who shout loudest usually get more of what they want

Tip No 12: Intervene early when things go wrong

Draw the line as soon as you feel uncomfortable

Tip No 13: Look for change and development

Notice the changes and differences

One of the things that people often comment upon, and which holds true in my experience, is how different individuals with Asperger's syndrome can be, even though the similarities are also obvious. It may help with understanding the condition to explore some of the ways of describing this. For instance there is a suggestion that a broad categorisation into three distinct groups within the syndrome can be helpful. Within the condition there are three notional groups: passive, aloof and odd, and active. These are rather arbitrary lines, but it is helpful to have the information that the groups exist. From my own position, I find passive people easier to work with (though slower), and I sometimes wonder if the work has any long-term effect. The active group tends to be harder to relate to, and I find myself trotting after them, trying to get some reflection into the work, while the aloof but odd group tends to make me feel a little overlooked and ignored: it seems to be difficult to have value for them.

Group 1 is passive, accepting social situations with indifference, often compliant and therefore vulnerable. These people may appear to enjoy social contact, but find it very difficult to make spontaneous approaches, and they may have difficulties dealing with stress and change.

Ravi, aged 34, spends his free time wandering the shopping centres of London. He has just moved into his own flat, having spent ten years in the psychiatric system. Over the past year and a half he has started doing adult education classes. After more than six months he has begun to talk within these classes. He met a woman who liked him, and whom he liked. He has her phone number; he has not called her. He moved into his flat eight months ago, and is still waiting for his father to show him how to use his cooker!

Group 2 is active but odd, seeing their own needs as the priority, with little interest in living communally, making compromises or seeking consensus. They often have little regard for social rules and norms, and they find non-verbal communication, as well as abstract or complex language, particularly difficult.

Simon lives alone, seeing only his mother and me. He does not like to go out because he thinks people look at him. He is black and dresses in a very noticeable way, including patent leather boots with thick wedgie soles. He is writing a sci-fi film script and thinking of moving to Turkey, where he thinks he will be more comfortable. He has no work and no Turkish language, though he has the money to buy a house he has found.

Group 3 is aloof, making overly formal and stilted social contact, preferring to be alone and sometimes withdrawing completely, perhaps even abandoning attempts to care for themselves.

George is extremely bright, and committed to an academic life in which he makes a significant contribution. He is looking forward to the point where humanity mixes with technology so that a qualitative breakthrough is made in human development. He has no qualifications, seeing A levels and degree work as so far beneath him as to be risible. He would only like to work with an eminent published astronomy academic. He recently set himself the target of learning the dictionary and its definitions. He lives in comparative isolation in a residential home, afraid of transport, heights and people.

Of course as soon as such a suggestion is made, exceptions come to mind, but this model is helpful to me because it partly describes how different individuals with the same condition can be. Another variation in the syndrome comes when not all three of the main points of the triad are present, or they are not present to the same degree: some people may be socially competent, or good conversationalists, for instance, and some may not exhibit signs of rigid thinking. There may be many of these people who have not fallen into the medical and social pathologically-orientated networks; they may never be diagnosed and consequently they may be denied appropriate help. I have a friend who coaches "difficult people" in business. She reports that if she is talking to a managing director or human resources director, they can immediately identify these people (low team ownership, marginalized and eccentric, low compliance with requirements that seem not to make sense, poor or unrelentingly high organisational standards, and general puzzlement about how they deliver such exact and precise work despite all of the above). "Sounds familiar?" she asked. "Sounds familiar!" I agreed.

Timothy is in his late thirties, employed as a technical editor in a scientific publishing firm. When I met him he was in trouble because of his social skills: he frequently interrupted people as they addressed their imminent deadlines in order to talk about his novels, cats and bread-making. He was in a special position in that everyone seemed to tolerate more from him than from others, recognising that he was different but not knowing how. He self-diagnosed as having Asperger's from the Internet.

Nigel is a director of an architecture firm. He is excellent in his area but fails to meet deadlines, is spectacularly untidy in his office, and finds it hard to issue invoices or arrange appropriate financial terms for new contracts. He does not contribute to board meetings, but often disagrees with the decisions arrived at afterwards.

If any of these traits go beyond a certain place, a diagnosis of Asperger's becomes less likely than perhaps one of obsessive-compulsive disorder or social communication disorder or semantic pragmatic disorder.

From the point of view of my work, in which I coach people to manage their life more satisfactorily, it seems clear to me that diagnosis is an imprecise art, and that some people can manage their life well enough to get by without special help whilst others cannot. A diagnosis is helpful inasmuch as it helps understanding and attracts support. In some cases the person does not fit the necessarily arbitrary lines around different conditions, but they still need to be recognised as a person who is in need of support, and they may still benefit from recognising that their neurology is somewhat different to the neurotypical group. In any case, it is more useful to enquire if a person will benefit from coaching than to require that the exact condition must be identified precisely in advance of any support being offered.

Timothy responded well to coaching in social skills, and learned to read the signs of a busy person—coat still over the back of the chair, papers all over the desk, text on the screen rather than news or cartoons, typing . . .

Some no doubt go ahead and create a satisfactory life, never coming to my attention. I hope there are many of them. Others crash out of the system, either because the condition is too strong in them to allow them to cope with everyday life, or because the bad experiences they have are too great for them to deal with. Whatever the outcome, throughout life it is far more likely that they experience a higher level of anxiety than is comfortable, and a confusion similar to that experienced by a tourist in a foreign country. Those who enter a relationship often experience their partner being dissatisfied because there is a lack of intimacy and a reluctance to experience new things.

> *Robert works for a successful advertising company, and reports that he never feels he has said what he really wanted in meetings. Girlfriends repeatedly complain about wanting more intimacy.*

This way of living obviously creates problems, but in some ways it might be easy to see that such a person could be accommodated and accepted by those around him. However, it seems that people with Asperger's often feel uncomfortable with themselves. Some report that being in the world is like being on the wrong side of a glass wall—frustrating. Others that they are so self-conscious that even simple things like cleaning teeth become conscious acts. Many are aware of their limitations and feel trapped inside their own nervous and obsessive selves. Depression is often a co-morbid feature, as are oppositional defiant disorder, antisocial personality disorder, Tourette's, attention deficit hyperactivity disorder, anxiety, bipolar disorder, obsessive-compulsive disorder, dysgraphia, dyspraxia, dyslexia, dyscalculia and dysphasia.

Tip No 14: Respect
Listen and let it sink in before you make suggestions or judgements—it is the other person who has to live his life

It seems to me that there is also a pattern of breakdown that occurs in some, though there is no study I know of that corroborates this. However, I see a pattern in which the young person sometimes holds on to his confidence for as long as possible, suffering the slings and arrows of particularly outrageous fortune as he washes though failure after failure, until finally he is unable to face any more and retires to his bed, from which he may well be taken to the psychiatric hospital for a while. There is a known correlation between Asperger's and mental ill health which may account for this, and it is quite possible that people recover even from apparently serious breakdowns.

Tip No 15: Work with the system
Diet? Sleep? Digestion? Medication? Relationships?
Environment?

After a long period of blackmail, Sean was beaten up, attempted suicide, and was discovered by his family, at which point his guilty secrets emerged. Having shared all his guilty secrets, he is now rebuilding his life and looking forward to returning to work.

There is an apparent epidemic of this condition, in which the number of reported cases has increased tenfold over ten years in the UK. Some areas in the US report higher increases. There is, of course, controversy over this, some suggesting that it is due to the measles-mumps-rubella vaccine (or the mercury-based preservative thimerosal which was used in it until recently), or, less scandalously, to the increasingly hostile environment into which children are born. This same environment appears to be responsible for the rise in asthma, nut allergy and eczema, and there is a theory that a genetically inherited weakness can be triggered by an environmental insult to launch a child into autism, so there is case to be made. However, others say that the increase is not real but is a product of greater awareness in schools and families which enables us to identify the children, and better diagnostic services which allow us to recognise them formally. Whatever the cause, it seems we can assume that there are about 1% of children with autism in the population, and that 60% of these will be affected by Asperger's syndrome, so we can work on the idea that about one person in every 170 is affected by Asperger's syndrome. We do not have the information to be sure if this is reflected in the adult population, which is harder to study than the child population. From my own experience I would suggest that people with Asperger's, left untreated or wrongly treated, can develop enough symptoms to justify a diagnosis of mental ill health and consequent medical intervention, which could mask the under-lying Asperger's syndrome. This is a contentious area, of course, and it is hard to achieve clarity.

I want to return to the idea of developmental disorder. All autistic spectrum disorders are classified as developmental disorders, which are birth defects affecting the child's ability to develop normally. In the case of Asperger's, it seems that the main area affected in this way is the social, and consequently communication. I note that the condition becomes self-perpetuating as the child grows: failure to communicate must breed a deeper fear of trying to communicate, an unwillingness that becomes part of the person as they find that their attempts to communicate do not bring them satisfactory results. It seems to me that this process will create learned negativity around the whole idea of attempting to make effective contact with other people, and that this secondary condition—learned non-communication—may well be more open to change than the primary neurological condition.

Tip No 16: Create powerful resource states
Do what you can to help the person feel good now

Hans Asperger was an Austrian paediatric psychiatrist, practising in his home town. He noticed a small group of children and wrote about them in 1944, only four years before I was born. He wrote in German, which may have been a problem as there was a war on. His work only became available in English when Uta Frith translated it in 1991, though Lorna Wing had been writing about Asperger's syndrome ten years previously, so it was not unknown. In 1981 or so, when I was a newly trained teacher and was teaching autistic children, we had a child referred to us. He was little older than most of our referrals, coming to us at the age of ten. I was about 33, and the syndrome was about 37. It was rumoured that Pete had Asperger's syndrome, and that was the very first time I heard the term. We had little idea, except that it was like autism but with normal IQ and good language.

Pete was tall and thin, with ginger hair and spots. He had a quiet voice, and seemed to be always laughing at us. Looking back, I would imagine that he was acutely embarrassed to be seen with the other pupils, who were autistic through and through. He used to spend a lot of time cracking sniggering jokes behind his hand, and swore a lot, as I recall. We were doubtful of our value to him and felt challenged, but looking back, it seems as though the school was the "least worst" alternative for him. The strength of the school was that we could give him a lot of individual attention, which we did, and he found a way to get along with most of us in his quiet and guarded way. He must be about 40 now, and is at the front of the epidemic. Over the intervening quarter century many more people have discovered the term, schools have been opened specifically for these children, and a library has been written describing the work which has been done in coming to understand the condition. Most of it was too late for Pete.

A number of individuals with Asperger's syndrome have written and spoken about their experiences: Ros Blackburn, Donna Williams, Temple Grandin, Lianne Holliday Willey, Claire Sainsbury, Wendy Lawson, Jane Meyerding et al, and Robyn Steward, who has her story up on her blog and is an emerging trainer in the UK. From this it seems that women with the condition may be in a different boat to the men—at least they can write about their experiences, though Luke Jackson has a go in his book *Freaks, Geeks and Asperger Syndrome*.

Tip No 17: Future pacing
Talk though the future in the present tense and pay attention to the response

Experience comes to us in little random bits, and we deal with this by using three tools (generalisation, deletion and distortion) to make sense of these bits and create patterns that we can handle as we go though life. These patterns are our beliefs. I remember my daughter watching out of the car window as we drove around the Hampshire countryside and commenting on the animals in the fields. First they were all "na-na", then they were all "orse", and so she went, noticing the defining details and learning the names attached to each sort of animal. All children who learn to talk go though the same process, as you did if you have read this far! At about the same time in her life I recall her walking carefully around the far edge of the room, pointing at the Aga and saying "'ot!" She was deleting the information that heat diminishes with distance. With the animals, she was playing with generalising (everything with four legs is a "na-na". No, they are all horses! No, the white ones are sheep!). In that process her generalisations were becoming more specific.

We all have to generalise and group our perceptions and experiences together, and this is one of the ways we form beliefs: "I went into a shop and felt uncomfortable because they ignored me, and I learnt to believe that I will always feel uncomfortable in shops." Or: "I once tried to sing and they laughed at me because I went off-key, and I learnt that I can't sing."

Tip No 18: Challenging negative generalisations
Reframe towards possibility

Will is frightened of people, believing that they are looking at him and seeing how odd he feels. He justifies this by referring to a group of kids who threw stones at him when he was in his twenties. He is now in his forties. He cannot abide traffic jams because he thinks other drivers are looking at him, nor can he walk towards a stranger knowing they will pass by each other in the street.

So with my daughter learning about the hot Aga, we had allowed her to feel how hot it was, and she had deleted (or in fact not yet learnt) that heat diminishes with distance, and so only felt safe if she was on the other side of the room (she has got over this now!).

We all also delete in order to find patterns that we can understand: "Mum went out!" or "Mum put her coat on, opened the door, came back for her bag, walked down the street, went to three shops . . ." and so on. In writing all this, I am getting over years of deletion when asked "what is Asperger's syndrome?" and only having a conversational time period of a few minutes in which to answer.

I can play the guitar and do so every chance I get, and could talk for hours about exactly what I enjoy and try to do when I am playing. "Can you cook?" requires deletions in order to answer yes, because if you consider questions such as "What can you cook? When did you cook last? What ingredients do you use for spaghetti bolognaise (for instance)? What shops you use? What do you consider is healthy food?" and so on, you realise that actually the question is more to do with "Do you believe that you can create meals?" or "Do you feel competent in the kitchen?"

Tip No 19: Challenging negative deletions
Reframe towards possibility

> *Simon believes people look at him, but has no evidence. He omits to notice that he is sometimes so tense that he runs down the street, looking as if he is trying to avoid attention, thus attracting attention.*

When my daughter was 13, she had the misfortune to have a bedroom next to the bathroom and to be experiencing adolescent hormonal changes. Whenever we flushed the toilet, she accused us of doing so deliberately to disturb her. This only lasted a year, and is a good example of the third mechanism, distortion, in which you connect previously unconnected things in order to make sense of your experience. People with Asperger's find this easy to do, as they tend to be internally rather than externally referenced (they get more of their information from their own internal experience rather than from what they can see, hear, feel, taste and smell), and will, for instance, think that when other people look at them they also judge them as odd-looking. We all do this, of course (I am in my fifties now and I have to accept being overweight despite my internal distortions of my body image), but people with Asperger's, in my experience, do more distorting and less generalising, thus creating a belief structure which supports the behaviour that gives rise to their diagnostic features in the Triad of Impairments.

Tip No 20: Challenging negative distortions
Reframe towards possibility

> *Ravi also believes people look at him, seeing that he is feeling odd. (This is common in Aspies.) He believes that groups of Asian men will jump on him at any moment. He thinks people see him and dismiss him as being a low-life. He once grabbed a man he thought was following him, because the man was behind him on a train station platform.*

Behaviour arises from belief. Sometimes this is conscious: people choose what they will and will not do. However, we all know that our thinking brain does not completely direct our behaviour, or there would be no smoking, overeating, rows, or forgotten birthdays. Much more usually, behaviour is patterned into the unconscious and we go on automatic pilot (think of driving, for instance). More usually, we live our life within our rather predictable patterns, choosing not to break laws, avoiding bungee and parachute jumps, eating a little too much sugar, trying to control our partner in life and making sure that we get a little more of everything than the other person does (or maybe that's just me!). People with Asperger's who become violent and break things when they are frustrated probably know that this not good behaviour, probably wish they didn't, but do it anyway, and so at some level they let themselves off the normal rules. I will explore this in more detail in Chapter Three. For now it is enough to establish that behaviour is connected to beliefs, which are formed from our perceptions about our experience, and it is in the perceptual and sensory mechanisms that Asperger's syndrome arises.

> *Robert walks about as though he is about to have a fight, wearing clothes that attract attention (designer labels, lots of torso exposed). He complains that people look at the back of his head, which looks normal— I looked. When I watched others, I found that one man did in fact look at him and give him a dirty look, though not to the back of his head but more to his overall presentation.*

CHAPTER THREE

How does it arise?

This is a condition that probably arises in the genes; it expresses itself though the personality in various forms of behaviour that give the diagnostician a chink through which she or he can see the condition at work. In fact it works on a number of levels, but it is only behaviour that is visible enough to be conclusive in diagnosis. New research is streaming out, and whilst it is pointing us in a direction, it is still far from clear about the destination. It does now seem clear that there is little expectation that one single cause will ever be identified. I won't go into exact detail about the research, as that would require a book of its own and would be outdated before publication, but there are some patterns which have been established by now and which are very helpful in understanding how this condition arises and how it exerts its influence.

Firstly, it is clear that there is a high rate of heritability, and the likelihood of creating Asperger's syndrome is enhanced if there is a history of mental illness, autism or learning disability in the family. However, nothing is certain in this area, and it seems that the condition can arise spontaneously. It also seems as though one mechanism for the condition to arise is that the inheritance is a predisposition which can be triggered by an environmental insult, which could include being dropped, a difficult birth, sudden shock, or presumably some ingestion of insulting environmental ingredients.

There is a variety of evidence that brain architecture differs slightly in Asperger's when compared to NTs. Some areas seem to grow faster than normal, some seem to be larger, some may be smaller. There is conclusive evidence that the communication within the brain is, in some areas, less strong than in an NT. Unsurprisingly, this is visible in brain scans when people are required to examine faces, something at which Aspies do not excel. They do not excel because while in an NT seven or eight areas of the brain become excited when confronted with a face and chatter to each other, in an Aspie only one area lights up for moment, bored or uncomprehending.

Annie is unable to recognise faces. She relies on identifying people's shoes, which she explains to everyone she meets. She does not make eye contact easily or notice others in the street.

Also, new research suggests that while feelings are the same, Aspie or NT, the ability to notice these feelings is diminished in some, and the ability to reflect upon them is diminished across almost the entire group. Thus if a person with Asperger's is asked to watch a video with emotional content, he will have the same feelings that an NT will have. However, an NT is more likely to be able to say "I feel sad when I see that", and an Aspie is less likely to be able to say "How strange that I feel sad when I see that". This is to do with brain functions in different specific areas which can be observed by use of a mfRI scanner. Uta Frith is currently researching these differences.

Tip No 21: Acceptance
Let him be for a while!

However, a strong part of the emotional mechanism lies in the blood chemistry and how the endocrine system works in secreting hormones. In fact, as Candace Pert discovered, there are receptors and secretion centres on all organs which add to the blood chemistry by exchanging short protein patterns called peptides (more than a hundred different varieties), and the resultant chemical cocktail gives rise to emotional experience, which is therefore apparently not the sole responsibility of the nervous system. On one level (in our guts or hearts, perhaps) we have always known this, but it is only recently that the evidence has been available.

Tip No 22: Uptime/downtime
Lead him to a better place

Tip No 23: Meditation
The single most important thing for you and the other person to learn

Tip No 24: Relaxation
When you feel you are about to lose control . . .

One of the first things I learnt about autism, and I am quite sure it is also true of Asperger's, is that people affected often tend to have unstable autonomic nervous systems. This system famously controls the fight or flight reflex, essentially by pumping large amounts of adrenaline out when required (or sometimes when not required). However, it also controls the cardiovascular system and all other automatic responses. If this is unstable, then fear of social expectation could be magnified, as could anxiety and obsessiveness.

> *Will hates sitting in traffic jams, fearing that people are looking at him as they wait to move. If they look at him, he believes, they will think he looks odd. When we drive into traffic he stops talking, looks straight ahead, and shows all the signs of panic. He asks me afterwards if I noticed anything, and wants to know that I saw how difficult it was for him.*

Scientists apparently find it difficult to talk across the disciplines—limited social skills, I suppose—and the gut scientists are not in close communication with the geneticists or the neurologists. If this is slanderous, I apologise; all I can say is that my information came from a scientist. Paul Shattock is a gut scientist in Sunderland University, and his research suggests that many (though not all) people with autism (and Asperger's) have a leaky gut, and their digestive system allows semi-digested material to permeate into the blood. In the case of casein and gluten, the semi-digested proteins mimic the opiate peptides and can flood the awareness receptors for these chemicals, interrupting our perception of pain and discomfort; this can lead to a blockage in the peptide system and an addictive state towards gluten and casein. Again, this eventually interferes with social interaction, because if you have a constipated emotional system, your empathy will be interrupted.

> *Pete is a young man I used to teach in the early '80s, who was very hyperactive and an elective mute: although he was able to speak, he didn't, nor did he appear to listen much. He used to spend his days at home going round the sitting room without touching the floor: sofa, table, TV set, window sill, door, table, chair, sofa. When his mother stopped him eating chocolate and took tartrazine out of his diet he settled down, discovered the floor, and began to speak.*

There is also a link between Asperger's and clumsy child syndrome, so another disrupted system may be the proprioceptive system which allows us to know where the bits of our body are in relation to each other. You may recall the difficulty that you or some of your friends may have had when as adolescents you went though a growth spurt. I grew from being a slightly large ten-year-old to being a six foot skinny eleven-year-old, so I do clearly remember how embarrassing and difficult it was to be clumsy and out of control of my body.

So our experience comes from our perception: in people with Asperger's, perception can be affected by the specific features of brain architecture or function, which can be exacerbated by the peptide emotional system and the digestive system working imperfectly.

There are automatic systems at work in our behaviour which will affect perception. When we NTs are with another person, we conduct a little dance called body language. Apparently robot scientists are trying to build robots which can replicate this, but are finding it difficult. Trying to analyse this non-verbal conversation is difficult; trying to teach it is even harder. My experience suggests that some people with Asperger's improve in their body language reciprocity when they are relaxed and familiar with the other person, but shut down amongst strangers. What is clear is that Aspies find it hard to do the dance correctly. Because of this, others become uncomfortable and conversation does not flow. If you compare this with supreme communicators such as Bill Clinton, who apparently makes everyone feel special, it is easy to see the gulf that exists and the effect that gulf can create. Embarrassed and uncomfortable situations abound with people who have Asperger's. This naturally impacts on their social life. The person with Asperger's sits still, looking ahead, not moving, speaking in a flat voice, and the NT starts trying harder to make him feel comfortable, probably overacting her own efforts at communicating rather than helping the situation by slowing down to his pace, thereby establishing a higher level of rapport. This is not a way to make friends. It is, in fact, a way to not make friends.

> *When I was first teaching, we thought it was a good idea to teach the class to do yoga. We spent the best part of a term teaching them to stand in a circle. After half an hour the concentration went, and usually we only worked at creating the circle. When we had that as a competency, we asked them to hold hands, and the circle dissolved as they moved away from the body contact.*

A specific piece of body language is eye contact. One person reported to me that eye contact felt like burning—he had to force himself to do it but it never felt comfortable for him. Some people do it in a fairly normal way, though these seem to be in the minority of the people I meet. Most do not easily make eye contact, or occasionally overdo it and stare continuously. Research suggests that a lot of people with Asperger's tend to watch only the mouth in conversation, not glancing at eyes, shoulders or feet. NTs, on the other hand, shift their gaze continuously to take in specific spots which enable them to remain aware of the whole upper body at least, but especially the eyes. Next time you are talking with a friend whom you don't mind offending a little, try just watching his or her mouth. When I tried it, I found that, like the people with Asperger's in the study, I lost the ability to know when it was my expected turn to speak, and also the awareness to know when to stop and pass the baton. I was short of information because I was not doing what I usually do unconsciously, which is to suck up information from the other person like a whale chasing plankton.

Tip No 25: Extra clarity from body language
Make your meaning clear

So with all these systems malfunctioning, the person with Asperger's forms beliefs about himself, and as beliefs direct behaviour, this is powerful. I have two cats, Madeleine and Pearl. Pearl is younger. She believes that she can go anywhere, but seems to know that Madeleine resents it. Madeleine, on the other hand, believes she can go anywhere, but not where Pearl is. Neither of them likes being in the same room, and wherever Pearl settles is where Madeleine can't go. Pearl believes she has free access to all the gardens and houses in sight, and happily walks across the roofs opposite, waving at me as she promenades a windowsill 20 feet up. Madeleine believes she needs permission to sit next to me. I could go on at length, but my point is that even cats act out of beliefs. For us, the human species, these beliefs are the most motivating things—people fight wars, leave each other and commit heroic acts because of their beliefs.

We build beliefs by experiencing patterns that make sense to us— it is only necessary in the UK to visit a pub on an afternoon when a football match is on to find out that beliefs have very little to do with the truth, but are still strongly held by individuals.

Tip No 26: Congruence
If you believe you can, you are probably right

Some of the beliefs that people with Asperger's may form will be affected by the patterns they perceive, and if their perception is wonky, the beliefs may not serve them. I will talk about family dynamics later, but it is very common for me to meet a young man with Asperger's syndrome who believes that he never has to cook, do the washing, or pick up his dirty clothes. In fact this belief is right, because all these needs are met by his parents. On a grander scale, it is easy to believe that as an Aspie you will never make friends, in which case you will not try. Some people with Asperger's, having spent a good deal of time alone, use their own imagination as the main source of their experience, and having come to believe that in a while everything will be all right, seem to find it very difficult to see that there are necessary steps in making even the simplest thing happen, let alone the move to having a wife, a job, a house, a car and two children.

Anger is a force that comes from the emotions: most of us learn to control it, but if you have no belief that you know what is going on, it is hard to do the necessary predictive work in order to manage your anger. You probably also have to have a belief that other ways of communicating will get you what you want faster or better.

Understandably, then, diagnosis is difficult. Many features of the person interact to produce the behaviour which has to be recognised and matched to the DSM IV by a qualified, experienced and open-minded diagnostician. At the last count, in the UK, the average age of diagnosis is 11. It seems to me that early recognition could enable us to offer better support in order to avoid all these negative beliefs being created, and so maximise the chance of satisfactory progress though life.

However, it may be good to keep in mind that Robert Spitzer, lately chair of the group which oversaw two out of five revisions of the DSM and defined more than a hundred mental disorders, has stated: "What happened is that we made estimates of the prevalence of mental disorders totally descriptively, without considering that many of these conditions might be normal reactions which are not really disorders. That's the problem, because we were not looking at the context in which those conditions developed." It seems that something may be awry with the diagnostic system he helped to invent, and whilst it is clear that Asperger's syndrome is a real condition, I am interested in the idea that much of it may be a normal reaction to abnormal circumstances.

CHAPTER FOUR

What do we currently know about this condition?

Medical science reduces things to their constituent parts and focuses on the problems. Although this can be useful, the treatments arising from this line of thought tend to be for the constituent or co-morbid conditions. This is reflected in how we work with Asperger's, and has interfered with the focus of how we help people live successfully with this condition.

Arguably, psychology began with Franz Anton Mesmer, who was born on May 23, 1734. He started out on his medical career by exploring how the moon and planets might affect our health: he was exploring the idea of tides within the body, leaning on Newton before him and Newton's friend Richard Mead. It has been suggested that Newton had Asperger's (but this is inconclusive and a complete irrelevance here, though interesting). Apparently he hardly spoke, was so engrossed in his work that he often forgot to eat, and was lukewarm or bad-tempered with the few friends he had. If no one turned up to his lectures he gave them anyway, talking to an empty room. At the age of 50, he had a nervous breakdown brought on by depression and paranoia.

Mesmer also met Mozart (who probably had Tourette's syndrome). Following a scandal resulting from an unsuccessful

treatment, Mesmer moved to Paris and explored "animal mag-
netism" ("animal" is equated here to using breath, not lustfulness)
using real magnets, and started on the road to hypnotism. Whilst I
am sidetracking, I find it interesting to note that some of his theories
seem to be close to the Eastern understanding of Chi energy, and
some of his ideas go close to R.D. Laing and homeopathy. He was
on to something.

The reason I start with Dr Mesmer and his technique of mes-
merising people is that he can be seen as one of the founding fathers
of psychology. The term was first used around 1500 by the Croatian
humanist Marko Marulić, and was popularised by Christian Wolff
around 1700. Philosophers and non-medical people worked on the
early ideas for about 170 years before Mesmer developed his techniques, which appear in retrospect to have been an early attempt to
reach the unconscious mind. Hypnotism followed, and medicine
advanced, though psychology remained largely philosophical until
the Germans began practical experimentation in the mid-1800s, a
time when physiology was also advancing. Freud began his case
study approach in 1890, and the unconscious was recognised, though
his approach was perhaps a little overly intuitive. So the new
discipline argued its way forward. In the USA, behavioural psychology was developed, using experiments on animals to define
approaches that would work with humans, and this was used to help
people to overcome unwanted behavioural patterns.

Of course the first thing to sort out was how the brain worked—
work that continues apace, and the early work refined our understanding of our perception and mental processes in a wonderfully
helpful way. Their work has entered the public consciousness
very deeply. In the 1900s, while Freud was doing his work, Gestalt
psychology was exploring how our perceptions affected our understanding; then behaviourism developed in the USA; Chomksy
challenged the idea that we are advanced animals and showed how
complex language development is, work which led to cognitivism
and the development of cognitive science; while Jung and Adler went
off in their different directions, Carl Rogers made his contributions,
and conditions arose that could light the spark for the age of the
individual.

In terms of coming to understand Asperger's, of course, it is
(even) more complicated than that. Psychology, psychiatry, neuro-

science, immunology, gastrology, psychoneuroimmunology and other disciplines, new and (comparatively) old, are all involved in trying to understand and support people with Asperger's. My point is that medical science understandably looks for what is wrong in order to heal it. Also, over the past 270 years, as knowledge has accrued and advances have accelerated, science has created many more branches, like an oak tree that would have spread its canopy over the same time period. As the acquisition of knowledge advances exponentially, it is not possible to do other than specialise, and this specialisation works against cross-discipline discussion. Apparently scientists don't talk across these borders because they don't speak the same language and rarely meet.

The Second World War rather interrupted the development of psychology and psychiatry: positive psychology was beginning before that time, and Abraham Maslow was in that particular flow, developing his hierarchy of needs and the idea of peak experiences and self-actualisation. Cross-border communication was interrupted; Dr Asperger's paper was written in the language of the military loser, to its detriment; and the focus on mental ill health prevailed to a large extent, just as the focus in Western medicine generally fell on physical ill health and the alleviation of symptoms.

So all these disciplines around human experience—physical, emotional, social, intellectual and spiritual—have developed rapidly since the Age of Enlightenment, itself partially kicked off by Newton, and because Asperger's syndrome manifests itself in all these areas, our knowledge and understanding is still fragmented. From the state of knowledge at this point, we can also be aware that we have so far been directed towards the pathology of what is wrong, at the expense of an exploration of what is and can be right. We can also surmise that there is a lot we don't yet know, waiting to be discovered.

We know more about what is wrong in Asperger's syndrome than what is right. What is wrong is enshrined and condensed in the Triad of Impairments, a hugely useful diagnostic tool which also contributes fundamentally to our understanding of this hard-to-grasp condition.

With a slightly different focus, we can also say that one of the main things wrong for Aspies is that the social world loves itself and hates outsiders. Without developing an understanding, we NTs can be naturally very condemning of Aspies, and this condemnation can in itself provoke some of the symptoms that demand treatment (anger, depression, withdrawal, etc). Things go wrong for these people without explanation and apparently beyond the laws of chance.

There is a big gap between the original neurological condition, the experience of the person affected, and the behaviours which consequently arise. Whilst some of the isolation and rejection can perhaps be put down to the original condition—inability to process body language makes other people uncomfortable—some of the behaviour arising can perhaps be attributed to negative experiences arising from this poor communication: "I just don't feel like trying any more."

Tip No 27: More acceptance
Give them good attention

To be repeatedly rejected from social situations in an obsessively social world must feel like discrimination. Jobs, relationships, friends, money: in Maslow's terms these are basic needs which must be met before self-actualisation can occur, and before self-esteem can be enjoyed. If we can see it as discrimination, then it is the responsibility of the strongest and most versatile to adapt—perhaps NTs can be taken further in their understanding of what they can do to accommodate the three in 500 people affected by this condition.

> *Annie needs a quiet place to work. If she feels it is at all likely that she will be shouted at, she cannot concentrate. She needs security away from sudden noise and smells. She can fix a computer or explain a system as well as the next person, and when she was at a well known IT warehouse, her sales figures matched everyone else's. When the manager shouted at her and told her how to do the job, her confidence crumbled and she had to leave.*

Moving the focus again, I can see that the limited support which currently exists for this group has been devised around the problems. Of course this is necessary and helpful, but it has taken energy away from the problem that concerns me, which is how to help people live successfully and independently with Asperger's syndrome. Residential housing exists for people who can't live effectively with their family or alone. Outreach is often a better solution, but again it exists to support people who can't quite cope. I don't want to dismiss it, just to note that we have only arrived at a staging post on our journey, not the final destination. Medication exists to quell anxiety, paranoia, phobias, depression, and so on, but at best only alleviates them. I have a great respect for medication, and fully acknowledge that it is necessary at times and can lead to the forma-tion of more positive beliefs, at which point it can be seen as a useful stepping stone. Some people will perhaps need their brain chemistry permanently adjusted. So long as side effects do not kill with kindness, and so long as the remedies are accessible to anyone affected by the condition, of course they are helpful.

It is not a criticism, nor a revolution, to suggest that there is now space for the emergence of some new work which will support people in discovering how to be more positive, accepting and powerful in their own lives. I have been finding my way forward in this for the past 17 years, using my initial training in neuro-linguistic programming as a starting point, and now, as I write this book, I see emerging corroborative features scattered though current academic and scientific work.

Rather than how pathological ill health occurs, positive psychol-ogy examines how wellbeing arises. We know that stress raises heart rate and blood sugar, and inhibits the immune response. We know that experiencing positive emotions (contentment, amusement) strengthens creativity, inventiveness and big picture focus. In response to the DSM (Diagnostic and Statistical Manual of Mental Disorders), positive psychologists are developing the CSV (Character Strengths and Virtues) to identify and classify positive psychological traits, including Wisdom, Knowledge, Courage, Humanity, Justice, Temperance and Transcendence. These are seen to be made up of 24 measurable character strengths. The push of this school is to support healthy people in becoming more healthy, so they are more effective. I believe that the US Constitution directs its government to support the pursuit of happiness. There are a number of ways being studied nowadays which give us the tools to follow this ambition.

Tip No 28: Create "feelgood"
Remember when we used to . . .

CHAPTER FIVE

Current support is poor

There are two separate issues in the difficulties people experience arising from the condition itself: other people's lack of understanding and inflexibility. The paucity of service provision arises from Government unwillingness which itself arises from the difficulties in understanding the condition. Current support is inappropriate and often inaccessible, and though people with Asperger's syndrome have undoubted abilities, they often experience difficulties in their lives which prevent them from using these abilities.

There is very little support for people with Asperger's syndrome. What there is tends to focus on the immediate problems rather than the longer-term possibilities of creating a solution. This arises from two causes: the scientific approach of cutting a problem up into ever smaller pieces in order to understand it, and the lack of political will to target this group early in order to avoid expensive crises. Asperger's only shows itself when the problems arise, and so the problems tend to attract treatment on the old pathological model. So we have behavioural techniques (quite useful in fact), medication and some extra attention, and advice given to those around the person on how to help them adjust and how to make the environment less of a threat and more comprehensible to them. As there are no dedicated budgets and these people fall between all the stools of mental health or learning disability, only those who demonstrate that they are having a sufficiently catastrophic problem are funded. So by the time you get to a specialist school or a residential home, you have had to demonstrate the necessity of that expensive funding. I think of it sometimes as qualifying: in order to qualify, you have to attract attention and make your case. In athletics you would have to pass the trials, run the early heats and stay out in front before you got the prize. Here you have to persist in demonstrating the extreme nature of your inability to live within the mainstream. There is very little support because although the potential demand is there, without money it does not generate action. Of course, by the time the qualifier gets the prize, a lot of damage has been done.

> *Maria is a young woman I taught for a brief time. She is autistic: high functioning, as they used to say. Although she regularly excluded herself from her classroom and watched the goldfish instead, she only got the attention that brought a new resource (me!) after she ran into the head's office and wrecked his notice board, then bit him. A qualifying move.*

Adult support services in the UK, despite repeated guidance from the Government, do not welcome Asperger's syndrome. The budget and organisation provides either for learning disability, defined by an IQ below 70 (excluding all people with Asperger's), or for people with a mental health condition, and Asperger's is not that either: it is a developmental disorder and the differences in aetiology, treatment, prognosis, consequent expectations and staff knowledge are profound. People with Asperger's are excluded unless they suffer from a secondary condition such as anxiety or depression, or put themselves or their families at risk. However, perhaps as many as 65% of people with Asperger's develop a mental health condition, and much of this will probably be because their condition is left untreated.

Anecdotal evidence suggests that a third of the UK's already over-inflated prison population is affected by this condition. If this is even remotely in the right ball park, apart from being shocking, it is a fair indicator that probation services are also pressured. So the criminal justice system is one default for people who fall through the community care net. Another is the mental health system, and whilst mental health community teams take on some very helpful work, there are also (probably) a lot of people with Asperger's syndrome who are sectioned under the Mental Health Act and held in psychiatric hospitals. Both of these options create a terrible experience, particularly for a person with Asperger's syndrome. In the case of the mental health system, use of the Mental Health Act often goes hand in hand with medication which carries side effects and addictive potential. If any of this human misery and substantial expense could be avoided, it should. In my experience it is clear that an episode involving a psychiatric hospital can define ten years or more of a person's life in an extremely negative way. Jail may be worse. The other default for individuals who fail to manage an autonomous life is the family, of course, but more of that later.

> *Victor was angry when a social worker visited and said the "wrong thing". He got a baseball bat and crashed it into a clock near his mother. The social worker panicked, not knowing Victor, and called the police, screaming attempted murder, despite his mother's protestations. Victor woke up three days later in hospital, strapped to a bed, with bruises all over him.*

The worst thing about these default solutions is that they are short-term and reactive, only alleviating the crisis by removing the person, who is then returned with substantial psychological damage sustained in transit.

The problem arising from all this is that the only people who are offered a service are those who have travelled so far down the damaging road of negative experience that they are already in crisis. By then the support they need is more intensive, the chances of it having a long-term beneficial effect are diminished, and the chances of co-morbid psychiatric conditions arising are increased.

Also, the support on offer is already defined and was designed largely for people with mental health needs: only cognitive behavioural therapy is of much use in the counselling department, and other services need to have a different dynamic and a different set of expectations which, if adopted, would make the service too expensive.

Specialist services are springing up, however. In the UK, the National Autistic Society is active in developing services; Brookdale Care is a privately run company with an excellent range of provision, and The Priory is developing a new project. I know there are many more; these are two examples I have personally seen. However, almost always these services centre on offering residential care. This is an expensive option, and if there is no local budget, this can prevent access through a "postcode lottery" effect. Also, services for people with Asperger's are always expensive because they are always staff-intensive. Despite the blossoming of so many services they are in practice still few and far between, so that potential users of such a service have to travel or have their lives disrupted by moving far from home, which does not support later re-integration.

However, despite services sometimes being inappropriate and arguably arriving at the party after the washing up is finished, there are waiting lists for them, which have the ultimate effect of maintaining a crisis whilst the potential service user waits for a place to become available.

In the world of education, things are very similar. The pupil is diagnosed at age 11 on average, and mainstream schools are encouraged to hold pupils as long as they can in the name of equality, so education authorities are reluctant even to consider private alternatives. The crunch comes at 13 or 14, when bullying peaks, and by the time the young person takes the matter into his own hands, often by refusing to go to school, it is too late to arrange an alternative and the damage is done, with the parents often taking some of the blame. The young person then retires to his bedroom and develops anxiety, or depression, or some other qualifying feature, whilst the family tries to manage their lives despite the gathering storm clouds. By the time the crisis strikes, he is past the age beyond which he no longer has a statutory right to education. Despite this, there are a number of schools specifically for pupils with Asperger's syndrome. For instance, in the UK the Hesley Group has a set of schools, and though they are all residential and extremely expensive, they also tend to have waiting lists.

Although there is also an apparent boom in the number of people recognised to have Asperger's syndrome in the UK and America, Australia and Japan, the situation is less clear elsewhere in the world, and this pattern may not be a universal phenomenon. The comparatively recent and currently expanding awareness of the condition, which may itself be responsible for this apparent epidemic, also helps to explain why such little effective support exists. Services have yet to catch up with this newly defined level of need.

So current support is inappropriate because it focuses on the outflow of a crisis rather than the pre-crisis person. Crises change a person's outlook on life, and the damage, once done, takes time and effort to repair.

For the most part, in the UK at least, if any support is forthcoming, it is usually mental health services which offer what they can to adults with Asperger's. The difficulty with this is that the dynamic in a mental health staff team is not appropriate to anyone with any form of autistic spectrum disorder. One of the first lessons I learnt as a teacher of autistic children is that you have to intervene, whereas it seems to my untrained eye that the dynamic in mental health work is far more *laissez faire* and accepting. It seems that at the least some of the work involves maintaining contact whilst the clients recover their equilibrium: a sophisticated waiting game, but nonetheless a waiting game. Life in a day centre revolves around a leisure ethos, smoking cigarettes and opting in to the occasional class or activity if it seems like a good idea at the time. This is unhealthy and confusing for people with Asperger's, as they often find it difficult to make choices and deal with free time, preferring to be task-focused and structured. Also, of course, day centres are peopled with clients who are suffering from mental ill health, and some people with Asperger's can be highly suggestible, which is an opportunity for a coach, but also for a paranoid schizophrenic.

Most current services tend to be not only inappropriate but also inaccessible. They are expensive, and are not judged by standards that apply to this group; instead they are compared to grossly unsuitable but nonetheless cheaper alternatives designed for other groups. They are also inaccessible because they are centralised. I understand that services have to be viable and so have to tend to centralise what they do. I know from personal experience how difficult and expensive it is to develop a more flexible service, as the population is essentially fickle and professionals find them stressful. Demand is hard to manage, contact work is a small percentage of the working day, and staff turnover is high. However, it is hard to access a service which is many miles away, especially if you have

Asperger's syndrome and hate travelling. There are also frequent issues with waiting rooms, buses, offices, appointment times and other simple logistical arrangements, which can put a service completely out of reach for a person with Asperger's.

> Will, at 45, is chronically anxious. It took me a year of persuasion to get him to contemplate asking to try some medication. We found a general practitioner who was the most flexible in town—Will could not manage the walk to the surgery, let alone spend any time in the waiting room. However flexible he was, the GP could not absolutely promise to be at Will's house between 1.30 and 2.30; because of this they never made an appointment and the opportunity was lost. A simple but potentially hugely influential intervention was lost to him because his day is so routine-bound that he could not wait around or tolerate an unpredictably early call from the GP.

None of this is meant to dismiss what is available, though I wish it were specifically designed for the needs of the group rather than being a set of round holes for a set of very angular and individual square pegs. What little there is on offer, though, is more suited for those who are not going to make it into independence, rather than the group who might, and I fear that many might have to qualify by falling gradually into the second group before being offered any support.

Normally under these circumstances, the people affected would gather together and form a pressure/support group, but because diagnosis is a hit-and-miss affair still, and because the condition is so inimical to social contact this does not happen, so the voice is not heard, although this may be changing as the Internet weaves itself into our lives.

What is needed is support which is orientated towards the individual, includes the family as the first line of support, is highly flexible, adaptable, accessible, affordable and long-term, and leaves a lasting impression. The purpose of this service would, of course, be to enable and encourage the person with Asperger's to make the most of his or her talent and ability whilst developing and maintaining the maximum possible level of independence.

Tip No 29: Freedom of choice
Just to remind you that you can do what you want in fact

CHAPTER SIX

We don't know what these people are capable of

Some people with Asperger's syndrome have achieved fame and fortune, and some of those don't want to be labelled as such. Given that they often have a high IQ and a logical mind, we can expect achievers. Given that their experience is so damaging, we can also expect underachievers.

> We are not born to suffer. We are born to thrive. If you live in a dry area and your garden receives little water, you plant plants which like dry soil. But when you are given a plant that likes wet soil, you don't kill it, you water it, you spend one of your 1440 minutes each day watering that plant. Because you know that given the right care, that little bit of effort can produce spectacular blooms. And so it should be with children like us. [Joshua Muggleton, age 17]

We only know about those people with this syndrome who feel bad enough to identify themselves. We can also see that these people have, by and large, had a bad time in life, and that these experiences will have created some psychological negativity. Those on a different part of the spectrum, or lucky enough to have found a niche, may not want to identify themselves as having Asperger's—there is little benefit for them in doing so. We do know that they often have a high IQ, sometimes extraordinarily high. I also know from my own experience that some have great ability to see though the mess we NTs can create around ourselves, and that many have an intense interest in other people. I have sometimes found myself wishing some of the Aspies I have met could rule the world! It seems that NTs are rather poor at it.

Of course, the stereotype is that of the geek sitting for long hours at his or her computer, understanding everything but not finding a useful outlet for that understanding unless it is IT-based, but that is a model of an Aspie succumbing to a problem. There may be other, more successful models to discover or create in which the person is using their aptitude and skills productively, and those around them are willing to bend a little and adapt their behaviour to make the social pressure manageable so that everyone gets along. We quite like eccentrics, and almost all the Aspies I have met seem to welcome, or at least accept, clear direction. Perhaps we could find ways to enjoy and tolerate their odd behaviour, to tell them what is expected if they fail to pick it up automatically, make an effort to include them at times and allow them to withdraw at others. Of course then we are into coaching those around the Aspie, which is a vitally important contribution to make.

Nigel is a disorganised but highly expert director of an architectural firm who does not like being told what to do.

Anthony is a precise and deadline-orientated banker who experiences stress from the strip lights and strange shift work patterns.

Timothy is a technical editor who finds it hard to know the difference between social and work times.

Stephen Wiltshire is instructive: he has an extraordinary gift, and was introduced to someone with the vision to offer to become his agent as for any other artist. He has since been to Camberwell College of Art, received an MBE, and has a flourishing career as an artist arising because of this different approach to his artistic abilities. Stephen is autistic, and very different to people with Asperger's, but he is a good example of how ability can be welcomed and accepted:

he was recognised as an artist with autism, not an autistic artist, and has flourished because of it.

The important point to keep in mind is that there must be many people living with Asperger's syndrome in a satisfactory way. It is still so difficult to get a diagnosis anyway, and if you are living at an acceptable or successful level, there is little motivation to seek one. Also, if you fall into the wrong sector of the helping professions (criminal justice, psychiatric or learning difficulties: currently there is no right place for someone with Asperger's), it may be that you are not diagnosed or are wrongly diagnosed. The condition has only been understood for a short period of time, and I know of many people aged over 30 who have only been diagnosed in the past few years, and who now often also carry the tag of schizophrenia. Prisons are reputed to be full of people with Asperger's, and in the past so have psychiatric units. This situation, arising from the late arrival of the necessary knowledge about the condition and the difficulty in recognising people who are affected, creates waste in financial terms, arising from the difficulty of working with people with this condition without understanding, and waste in human terms of avoidable outcomes that magnify the problem without addressing any solutions. Although the situation is improving, and those leaving school who were diagnosed early are more aware, more assertive and better equipped, this group is disgracefully under-supported, both in childhood and in adulthood. Because they are so vulnerable to the actions and attitudes of others and yet so close to being able to live independently and satisfactorily, it is even more important that they are supported in a way that helps them to operate successfully in this world.

There are probably many people who are undiagnosed. Some of those will be living perfectly happily, perhaps working in a rule-governed job in which they are allowed to work on their own projects at their own pace and there is not too much emphasis on teamwork. They will perhaps bring an unusual level of focus, memory, intelligence and logic to their work, and will need minimum management, so they can be very attractive employees. If they have a relationship, it will probably be of the traditional model in which the woman manages the home whilst the man earns the money. The people working and living with Asperger's may experience a range of problems arising from the behaviours defined in the Triad.

It is likely that those around them will cover for them to an extent, preventing the true picture from being easily recognised. Controlling behaviour, incompetence with money and strangers, strange habits and difficulty with coping with change can all be covered for by other family members, as can a quite high level of violence. Recently, for instance, a pattern was recognised in which some women were realising that they had married a man with Asperger's syndrome and were seeking help for the first time, after years of marriage.

Many people with Asperger's syndrome are succeeding now, and some, as we have noted, succeeded in the past. It is a reasonable assumption, in my view, to say that we do not know what individuals are capable of, although of course it is not true to say that they are all capable of extraordinary achievements any more than it would be true of the NT population. However, I often realise that I have spent long hours working with someone to move beyond the disappointments and defences built up though the past years before we can actually get to grips with the condition itself. Occasionally I notice the condition showing itself, but usually it is hidden behind learnt negativity.

I don't want to give the impression that this is easy either. I remember George, with an IQ of 150, sitting in his room in a Brookdale House, convinced that he was about to make a major contribution to the world through his understanding of astronomy if only we could arrange for an eminent professor to come and give him private seminars. He knew a lot, but was unwilling, perhaps unable, to follow a course of study. With no school certificates (GCSE or A level) he found the idea of doing a degree to be irrelevant. His fear and his low opinion of himself were stopping him from even starting, and his fantasy was that he could leapfrog the whole of academia to become a significant contributor. Individuals like George, who was almost incapable of going out due to his difficulties with cars, buses and people, are not always ideal representatives, and I certainly would not say that I know better than those who had helped him to grow to the age of 20. It seems that some people with Asperger's are probably not strong enough to create an autonomously independent life. However, bad experiences certainly played a part in George developing his low self-esteem, phobias and fears.

I also note that Sir Patrick Moore, CBE, HonFRS, FRAS, and our well-respected TV astronomer, is self-diagnosed with Asperger's, has no formal qualifications, and yet was asked by NASA to help design work around mapping the moon. The Soviet Union also used his maps in the 1950s in their own exploration of the moon. It is a sidetrack again, but interesting, that he published (under a pseudonym) a book called *Bureaucrats: How to Annoy Them*. We don't know what people are capable of, and we can never know, of course, what might have been.

Sir Patrick Moore is one who happily owns up to thinking he has Asperger's. When you "deep Google", many suggestions emerge which link other known people to the condition. I have found Peter Sellers, Gordon Brown, Andy Warhol, L.S. Lowry, Bill Gates, and David Gilmour of Pink Floyd . . . let alone the Royal Family! This can be mischievous, of course, and perhaps if they are not having a problem (and only Peter Sellers and perhaps Lowry in that list could be said to have Aspie-like problems) then it is not necessary to recognise the condition.

Only a few people get to be famous, though, and my concern is more to really recognise that there must be many people out there who are affected by this condition, even if only lightly. Some of those will be succeeding, while others may not be achieving their full potential. The purpose of recognising this is only to reinforce my premise, which is that we don't know what these people are capable of.

> *Annie is developing her skills as film-maker and trainer, and is seeking publishers for her college work.*
>
> *Simon is developing a sci-fi film script and starting a sci-fi film club in London.*
>
> *Jamie is writing a computer game-based novel in preparation for his major fantasy trilogy, which he hopes to complete within the next ten years.*

All our information comes from the pathological end of the experience, and is weighted towards expecting people with Asperger's syndrome to have limitations and consequent problems. Some do; some problems may be unavoidable, and some could perhaps have been avoided with different formative experiences. Positive psychology suggests that we could do well to explore how those people with this condition who do move forward and use their creativity in their lives achieve that. Information on this is naturally very hard to collect, and maybe we have to make the jump towards NTs and ask the same question, then translate the answer back to the experience of the Aspie. That is what I am trying to do in some of my coaching. In neuro-linguistic programming terms this is called modelling.

Modelling is to some a definition of what NLP is all about: uncovering what processes a person uses to achieve something in a way that can be learnt by another person. I make the assumption that Aspies probably operate in a similar way to NTs. They have perceptions arising out of their five senses which they attend to (or not) and which generate responses—feelings and thoughts. They seek to make sense of this by creating patterns that group together some experiences, assign meaning to others, and ignore certain features in order to create seeming logic. Explaining NLP takes a while, and a library of work exists which explains it much better than I am able to do here (though there is more later), but what I have just described is a way of understanding how we all work. Aspies use this mechanism in different ways because of their different perception and different internal responses, but I believe the mechanism they use is the same as it is for all of us.

Tip No 30: Sensory future pacing
Create a "future memory"

Asperger's syndrome is a neurological condition. It creates difficulties in social relationships and communication, and people affected tend to be less flexible than others in their thinking. However, it is also associated with logical thinking, a quick grasp of complicated systems, high levels of intelligence, focus, compliance with procedures, attention to detail and high language skills. Pub talk suggests that some careers are full of people with Asperger's—engineers, computer maintenance and programming, any uniformed service, the civil service and local government, proof reading, research science, book-keeping and accountancy, library work—there are many jobs in which Asperger's can actually become an advantage.

However, this is a two way street: those around the person might be able to adjust in order to make it easier for him. The United Nations suggests three levels of definition: an impairment is the source condition, which can create a disability in terms of interfering with normally expected function. The handicap comes from the disadvantage arising from the disability. This is easy to understand if you imagine a person with cerebral palsy: the impairment is in the neural mechanism that controls the muscles. Because of this the person cannot walk and is forced to use a wheelchair. One of the arising handicaps is that they cannot use stairs or public transport, or get into many shops.

With Asperger's, there is a neurological impairment which gives rise to the Triad of Impairments (in this context it would properly be the Triad of Disabilities). The handicap arising is that relationships and communication go wrong, resulting in the secondary disabling pathology of anxiety, depression, etc. This is a little simplified, of course, and does not even consider that anxiety or depression may arise directly from the initial impairment. Simon tells me that I am one of very few people on the planet with whom he can feel comfortable and talk. This is because I make the effort (skills, knowledge and experience help me, of course). Other people could also make the effort and significantly improve the chances of people with Asperger's syndrome. However, the Aspies I meet have depressingly similar stories of confusion, fear, bullying, exclusion, failure and subsequent depression, and (even at best) underachievement.

I also have to mention here that I have seen the level of creativity that some of this group exhibit: it would be interesting to see if this is above the usual level. My personal theory is that if communication is hard, a pressure to express yourself may develop. If you are less aware than some about what others may feel about your work, you may feel more free to put your ideas into action without diluting them in order to please. I know of one aspiring astronomer, a student who is developing a video-based resource pack to help Aspie students move through college, a man who wants to move to Turkey, a novelist, several musicians, several artists, and a photographer. The creative act may be more attractive to them, but of course the networking that is attendant upon successful marketing is another story, which is why I mentioned Stephen Wiltshire earlier. Without the sympathetic, professional and radical approach of treating him like an artist, he could be unknown today, joining the ranks of underachievers who underachieve because they can't find a way to use their skills and talents.

Genes direct the body to grow in particular formations. If there is one or (more likely) several combinations of Asperger genes, then the direction is for the brain to grow or to interconnect in some slightly different ways. All I need to say here is that the vast majority of NT body tissue is identical to that of an Aspie. We have looked at how the condition arises and how the fundamental impairment gives rise to a more visible disability, which may then be a factor in the development of a handicap, in the UN's terminology. Leaving aside the genetics, which, though fundamental, are only the blueprint for the organism, not the thing itself, it is evident to me that people with Asperger's are much like the rest of us. We all see, hear, feel, taste and smell in the same way. Some Aspies are hypersensitive to sensation, although it is not the mechanism that is different, as far as I know, only the interpretation of the raw data from the sense organs. Some Aspies also seem to be able to be selective in their attention, again a difference in the perception of the sensation.

In terms of motor control they are identical. In appearance they are identical to us NTs. They seem to have the same mechanisms for cognition, memory, feeling and so on; it is the interpretive or attentional properties of the brain that may be different. This leads me to some ideas which are exploratory rather than research-based. In general terms, people with Asperger's work just the same as us. I feel as though I have said enough about the idea that the fundamental impairment gives rise to learnt negativity, but having just reminded you of it now, perhaps it is acceptable for me to use the notion one more time to restate that learned negativity is just that and no more. We all suffer from it at times, some of us being affected more strongly than others. Bad experiences teach us to be negative, and sap our power.

Brain plasticity is the feature of our neurology that allows the brain to relearn after, for instance, a stroke. Speech, or control of one side of the body, is lost because of the damage caused to the brain in the stroke, and over time, with help, the patient can use the other side of her brain to direct these functions. New parts of the brain take on speech or movement. Once a teacher always a teacher, I suppose, and so I sometimes find myself wanting to ask the researcher if an impairment in the brain could perhaps be overcome by using the plastic brain to allow one to learn to do something using a different set of tools. Of course there is no definitive answer, and researchers are very properly unwilling to speculate beyond their specific study.

Teachers, however, ask more dynamic questions: "How can I help him to learn that?" Questions that lead to new strategies being devised are usually helpful. In NLP it is recognised that "the map is not the territory". Obviously it isn't—what we mean in NLP-land is that the experience of something is not the thing itself, and can be changed. For instance if a smoker is denied his cigarettes, he gets anxious or frustrated or devious. This does not have to be so. The territory is "no smoking". The map is "dammit, no smoking!"

> *George could not abide heights as he had fantasies of throwing himself out of the window. In a secluded room on the fourth floor of a big house with high windows he was as comfortable as could be, enjoying the view over the park nearby.*
>
> *Will gets very anxious in public. Yolande invited him to come to her house one Sunday and he travelled across Central London on the Underground system because he liked Yolande. He punched someone on his return journey.*

These and many other examples tell me that this rigid thinking is possible to circumnavigate. Once you begin to ask how something can be made learnable, you increase your chances of discovering a strategy that works. So learnt negativity can be circumnavigated or relearned as proper caution in new circumstances.

My impression is that people with Asperger's syndrome undertake their perception and the formation of their beliefs and understanding in just the same way as the rest of us, and are open to new learning in just the same way. The big difference I perceive is that, either from the condition itself or from the strength of the previous negative experiences, they need mega-doses of positive experience to combat their existing negativity. One person with the condition described looking within himself as "staring into a big black hole". Whilst this is poetic and individual, many people have agreed with it, and it seems to me to be different from the NT experience. Without much ability to see inside yourself (though this may also be teachable), it is probably harder to move from negativity to a more positive frame of mind. How do you give yourself a good talking to, or monitor its effectiveness? So, like most of us, they perhaps notice bad experiences more than good ones, but maybe even more so. My experience is that conversely, they need mega-doses of good experience before changing their beliefs, under-standing, and therefore their behaviour. However, what they need mega-doses of is the same medicine that we all need.

I always feel better after talking with you. [Ravi]

CHAPTER SEVEN

We know that bad experiences generate negative psychology

In terms of learning about life, there is no significant difference between Aspies and NTs. In both cases, bad experiences lead to bad psychology. Aspies have many real reasons to be frightened, depressed, unwilling to try, dreamy, isolated, off on their own.

In the UK, the average age of diagnosis for someone with Asperger's was at the last (quite recent) count 11 years old. One of the reasons for this is that it is difficult to identify a young child with the condition, though I do in fact know of several who were diagnosed at or around the age of five; others I know had to wait until they were in their thirties. A social and communication disorder only shows itself in situations calling for social and communication skills, which develop as the young child grows and learns from experience. It may well also be true that some people with Asperger's have a weakened sense of themselves compared to us neurotypicals, but it is also self-evident that they share the mechanism we all have that allows us to learn from our experience. Of course, they have slightly different experiences arising from their perceptual and neurological idiosyncrasies, and so what they learn may be a little different to what the rest of us learn.

We know from all that has passed since Sigmund Freud trod the boards that people's attitudes and beliefs are formed in the light of their experience, and that people lose some of their power as they pass though the exposure time of childhood (the best days of your life) and adolescence, and develop into adults. I am pointing out the obvious fact that people with Asperger's have exactly the same mechanisms as us NTs and so there is access to tried and tested remedies, although they may need amending to suit the particular needs of this population. However, we do know that traditional talking therapies, especially the more psychotherapeutic ones, fail them badly. Cognitive behavioural therapy, only a sniff away from neuro-linguistic programming in its theory, does the best. This suggests that people with Asperger's have some difficulty in making those conceptual abstract inner links that help us to rejig our under-standing of ourselves. We know that they prefer concrete thinking; and linking thoughts and feelings with behaviour and focusing this on a specific goal is an accessible process, which can be learnt as a skill and hence evaluated in a concrete way. CBT will be the best solution for some—its disadvantages, though, are that it is limited to a relatively short series of sessions and only allows limited levels of connection between client and therapist.

It is also possible, through talking and through having new experiences framed in reference to past ones, to facilitate people in cleaning out their emotional and conceptual store cupboards so they can rediscover their passions and energy, renewing their confidence and focus and helping them to overcome the energy drain of being in two minds. There are several libraries full of theories about this, and I take the functional line that people respond well to discovering that life can be more pleasurable. In essence that is what directs learning: you move away from discomfort and towards comfort. Of course it is more complicated than that, so I will share a few examples:

Paul was a highly-strung youngster of about eight when I met him— I was his teacher. He used to talk the hind leg off a donkey (a figure of speech meaning that he talked incessantly until those around him were exhausted). People stopped listening after a time, interrupted him, and tried to redirect his thoughts, as a lot of his talking was repetitive and predictable. Also, the more he talked, the more excited he got, until he went out of control—not a pleasant experience for him. I began to teach him to write, which was not easy, as he found concentrating difficult (too much talking going on). I remember that a member of staff asked me why I was teaching Paul to write when there were so many other practical things he needed to learn, and although it seemed so obvious to me, I recall being a little unsure that I had a good answer. As soon as he got the hang of it, which did not take long, he spent hours writing what he had previously been saying. This was not a perfect solution as we still had to distract him from his thoughts and bring him into contact with others and the pressures of the world, but it seems to be a clear example of someone learning something because it was a better alternative for him than his previous behaviour.

I always clean my teeth night and morning because it feels good.

When I play the guitar I sit up straight so I can reach and have maximum range to flex my podgy little fingers.

I only nearly got run over once or twice before I learned that looking left and right is a good idea.

These examples are about the acquisition of useful skills. It is more comfortable for me to be good at playing the guitar than it is for me to slouch around whilst playing. My pupil saw the value of writing straight away.

Tip No 31: Talking up through the logical levels
So all parts of the person get the message

However, we are a dissatisfied and creative species. Most people want to move forward to achieve and acquire. The discomfort often comes from our wanting something we don't have, and in my experience the things people with Asperger's want are the same as the rest of us: a job, enough money, people around, a partner, and so on. It may be useful to refer to Abraham Maslow's concept of the hierarchy of needs at this point: the notion is that we need to meet our physiological needs before we can really attend to our need for security, which in turn enables us to work on meeting our needs for love and belonging, then self-esteem, and finally self-actualisation. This suggests that some of the dissatisfaction we can experience, and which people with Asperger's wrestle with, may arise from our lack of success in moving higher up the pyramid.

Whilst a lot of my work is focused on the first two levels, much of the difficulty seems to me to arise from my clients' difficulties in developing self-esteem and confidence at the higher levels, and it is at the third level that the social and communication disorder is at its most powerful as a saboteur, threatening to prevent access to these higher levels.

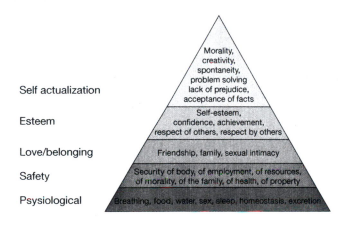

Self actualization

Esteem

Love/belonging

Safety

Psysiological

Morality, creativity, spontaneity, problem solving lack of prejudice, acceptance of facts

Self-esteem, confidence, achievement, respect of others, respect by others

Friendship, family, sexual intimacy

Security of body, of employment, of resources, of morality, of the family, of health, of property

Breathing, food, water, sex, sleep, homeostasis, excretion

What does not seem to be proven, though, is that people with Asperger's are cast in a mould that necessarily features negativity and poor ability to get things done—it seems more likely to me that some members of this group just give up trying when they repeatedly find that things fail to work out the way they want, and that this giving up is a source of the frustration, anxiety, depression and withdrawal.

Making things happen is at the core of coaching, of course. It is primarily a goal-orientated process, and the assumption is that you can learn new strategies for increasing your success rate. Goals can be external (playing the guitar) or internal (feeling satisfied), and it is possible to formulate goals at all levels of Maslow's hierarchy. However, we are all connected, and making things happen is almost always a process that involves others in one way or another.

Tip No 32: Leading the change process
Experience what you want the person to experience

Tip No 33: Parts work
When you are in two minds, you can talk to both parts of your mind separately

Tip No 34: Position change
Get up and move about

In my own coaching I find that focus on a goal is helpful, as is a massive overdose of positive attention (Carl Rogers' unconditional positive regard), a low pressure environment, and a sense of enquiry that links me to the client. It is not that they cannot rejig their understanding of themselves (I have met so many who have rejigged themselves into utter hopelessness, for instance). It is more that they need specific techniques that match their specific inner experience. Of course success breeds confidence, and one way of moving forward is to experience success, so I often try to encourage clients to develop small-scale goals in small steps to maximise the chances of success.

Tip No 35: Time frames
Be clear about the time frames and help the person move into the mid term

Tip No 36: Time lines
Let them explore the future by moving through it

There are strong repeating patterns in the lives of people with Asperger's—bullying in the early teens, rejection, repeated unsuccessful effort, unemployment, absence of friends. Many of these experiences arise from the social and communication disorder, and it is not difficult to see how they can give rise to the psychological profile we often associate with Asperger's syndrome, which includes a sense of being isolated, loneliness, fear, anxiety, lack of motivation and depression.

Annie was locked in the toilets at school and laughed at. She found her name scrawled over the bus shelter in the village where she lived. Another student now feels it is OK to shout at her, banging on her door at 8.30 in the morning. She has cerebral palsy, hemiplegia, dyslexia and many more conditions, as well as Asperger's. She was premature, went though an autistic phase, was late with all her milestones, and can't walk straight if she gets tired. Organising an evening meal is a big deal for her. She is about to go to university, and is worried that she won't make friends because she has learnt from these experiences that people are unfriendly.

Bernard has been overlooked and turned down so many times by his local authority in his efforts to get some support that he can't be bothered to ask them any more.

Nancy has got herself a place at acting school, and is desperate to lose weight so she won't be noticed when she gets there.

Harry nearly qualified as lawyer, but fell into a depression when he failed (only one section), and now finds it hard to do anything more than go to the pub in the evening and drink too much.

All of these responses arise from earlier experience, and all reflect a wider pattern amongst this group of people who seem to have ample reason to be depressed, anxious, lonely and so on. They also have very real reasons to be frightened of the future. Annie doesn't like to be responsible in case she messes it up. Ravi let his father order all his furniture when he moved into his own flat because his father knew what he was doing—Ravi denied himself the chance to learn because he feared he might mess it up. Simon wants to start a sci-fi film club, and though he is being lent films to show and knows what he is doing, when he tried to negotiate a venue he got two completely contradictory messages from the manager, and lost heart.

Tip No 37: Reassurance
Let the unconscious mind attach the required meaning

Tip No 38: Find the cause—Trans Derivational Search
Just ask and listen!

For all of us, fantasy is a great escape from the hard grind of reality. I am enjoying writing this book, dealing only with my own thoughts rather than having to grapple with creating value for a client or Hoovering downstairs. I can just live in my head for a while, as we all do when we sit on the bus, lie in a hot bath, or daydream our way through a meeting or lecture. It is more of a challenge to make a plan and make it happen, dealing with all the real things that get in the way, so I have to sit down and make sure I move forward in my writing plan. To move forward we need to keep motivated and keep alive to how our actions create consequences, adjusting as we go, so we circumnavigate problems without losing our sense of direction.

Tip No 39: Repetition
Three times at least!

Unless we can access the necessary resources to deal with problems, then the more uncomfortable reality is, and the more we are likely to withdraw into fantasy (thoughts, daydreams, plans). People with Asperger's have ample reason to be uncomfortable with reality. Coaching is a process of facilitating them in thickening their skins (success breeds confidence), sharpening their saws (skilful action is better than unskilful battering), persevering (never give up), and evaluating. (Am I getting there? What do I need to adjust?)

Tip No 40: Failure as feedback
Keep the door open—learn from everything

Attitude and belief, including negativity, is learnt from experience, though there may well be a pattern in Asperger's that makes negative thinking more likely than is the norm. In extreme cases, people can fall over into mental ill health of one sort or another, and this often brings them to the attention of the health services (if they are lucky). However, the crisis can obscure the solution in that it attracts all resources to the short-term goals of managing (for instance) depression at the expense of the longer-term goal of creating confidence, happiness and self-esteem.

Tip No 41: Reframing
Look at it another way—a better way

So the focus of the work I do is to address the underlying features that allow the more immediate crisis to arise. Because of the strength and importance of the work which has been done on mental ill health, where lives often hang in the balance, it has taken a long time for the positive psychology approach to emerge. Humanist psychology arose from the work of Maslow and Rogers in the 1950s, building on the earlier existentialists who thought that the individual creates his own reality. To cut a long story short, there is now an endeavour to explore how happiness works and how it can be created and enhanced. I say this because this is the opportune moment to note that there is an emerging academic background to the practice of coaching, although it is one I have noted rather than specifically explored. I base my own continually developing practice more in NLP, a practical and accessible technique-driven approach. More prosaically, and perhaps more accessibly, the tools of personal development are worth exploring, and I suppose the previous New Age movement is also worth waving at in friendship: it is a popular movement which is in synch with the more rigorous academic developments.

We are interested in finding ways to feel better about ourselves. Early developments in psychology and psychiatry naturally focused on helping unwell people to get well, and perhaps that hard task gave rise to a natural cynicism which is still abroad and which is unfortunately associated with consideration of the soft targets of happiness, self-fulfilment, love and vulnerability.

A few years ago I was at an NLP conference, and in her keynote talk, Shelle Rose Charvet suggested that we are now finishing the IT revolution. Although its effects are busy transforming our lives still, the initial revolution is over in that we have all come to terms with the omnipresent digital portals that are crowding around us nowadays. Further, she suggested that the next revolution, coming fast, will be the soft one of relationship and communication. Whether or not this is true remains to be seen. What is true in my experience is that there are established ways to remediate negative thinking, some of which go directly towards the creation of positive thinking. It also seems that sometimes these are seen as flaky in some way as the cynics have their say.

However, the developing and highly relevant school of conflict resolution is concerning itself with peace building strategies. Learning taken from political conflicts is being applied to communities under pressure in order to avoid future problems. South Africa has developed the Truth and Reconciliation process, which is extraordinarily unlike what went before. Maybe the cynics are about to learn something new.

Prime amongst the starting points for coaching is the positive statement which clearly articulates what you want. This gives direction to the work much more effectively, and is a creative act rather than the destructive and unfocused one of wanting to move away from some negative experience. You might think this is easy, and indeed there are some excellent structures which offer clarity and completeness in this definition, but if someone has experienced enough bad moments to create a raft of negative thinking, they often find it difficult to set their sights forward, and then they often look far ahead, and classically find it even more difficult than the rest of the NT world to develop and adhere to an effective strategy to get them from A to B.

Tip No 42: Well formed outcome
Clear and controllable, worthwhile and believable

Tip No 43: Outcome framing
"So what would it be like if . . . ?"

There is also the fine judgement about realistic or fantasy goals. I have accompanied Will on his journey for 17 or 18 years now, and he started out with a stereotypical desire to have a woman, a car and a job. Over this time he has been so affected by his social anxiety that none of this has got one bit closer, and although he is bitterly disappointed, he will now settle for much less. His anxiety prevented him from following a mid-term strategy. However, he will now settle for less, and maybe at the lowest end of aspiration it is a justifiable goal for someone to come to terms with their limitations and accept their life as it is, although this is highly subjective, and so is a hard goal to measure.

You cannot know what you can achieve unless you try everything you are capable of. When you have tried, you can then assess and come to terms with your self, although of course it is important to decide whether you want to pull out all the stops or not, and to calibrate your effort accordingly. So although it is better to set a small and achievable goal, it may be that the person wants to go further. Who are we to say what is fantasy and what is achievable? Simon wants to live in Turkey, which I think is highly risky, and all I can do is encourage him to examine the ramifications of such a move, and help him to examine his motivation—does he just want to escape from a difficult situation here, or are there more positive reasons for going over there? Will he be in a better situation over there than he is here?

So coaching in itself is straightforward in many ways: choose a positive goal, make sure you really want it, create a strategy for getting it that includes your internal essence and your external behaviour, and progress with regular checks and reviews. In detail, this process looks like this:

1. Set a goal and choose to make an action plan.
2. Prepare a plan with a route map that gives you milestones, awareness of the risks, the skills you need, supplies and emergency plans, short cuts, pit stops, companions and fail-safe mechanisms.
3. Do an "idiot check" internally and externally, make sure the plan is as good as it can be and that the ambition is sound.
4. Choose to make it happen.
5. Follow the plan, constantly reviewing, until you get to where you want to be.

Would that it were so simple! Of course it is more complicated, or we would all be rich, famous and pretty, and I would be a really good guitarist. Later I will go into more detail about this process and complicate it a little more.

The internal state of mind and body is the key to effective action: when you feel like doing something, you do it; when you don't, it can be really hard work. Being miserable at a party is a nasty experience, whilst being happy and sociable is a lot of fun.

I find that it can take a very long time before trust is created and a person is ready to explore the reality of their feelings. In that period of time goals change, short-term things get in the way, and there is a lack of focus. However, this is a preparation stage which aims to lead the person to acceptance of their past and present circumstances. Some of these circumstances are external (I have no qualifications); some are internal (I think they are all looking at me). This is helped enormously by a process of separating the facts from the feelings and opinions, and openly discussing these formulations.

Tip No 44: Separate feelings from thoughts
Separate fact from fiction

An important part of this stage is to accept that the person does want something and that there is a gap between the present situation and the desired one. This can be a hard thing to do as it implies dissatisfaction and failure. However, when you have accepted that, it is easier to accept the need for action.

Tip No 45: What do you want?
Back to basics

Also, frustratingly, there may be skills to be learnt before you get going, and it is probably natural for people to want to get on with their journey rather than hang about learning skills. Most of these skills are internal and ephemeral: when you can exert some control over your internal state, you can direct your thoughts and choose how to feel, thus affecting your behaviour automatically. Of course that behaviour is all the more impressive because it comes directly from you rather than from acting. Ravi now feels that he has the skills of breathing and talking to himself to prevent him from drifting off into a fantasy of violent thoughts and paranoia. He knows there are always things he can do to keep himself feeling positive and connected with the world, and he knows when and how to escape difficult situations without drawing attention to himself. He is currently settling into an adult education course about logic and philosophy, and for the first time in nearly 20 years he has a good friend with whom he goes out and about most days.

Wanting to give a couple of clients the tools to feel good and to flirt when called upon to do so, I gave them each a pebble. We then identified the states that help when you want to feel flirty (sense of humour, confidence, sensitivity, high energy, etc). I took each of them and asked them to re-experience a time in their lives where they felt each of those states. If they had no historical reference experiences, I asked them to imagine. As they experienced this state I asked them to feel the pebble. At end of the series of exercises, I asked them to hold the pebble and experience the cocktails of all the flirty feelings. We all laughed uproariously. They took the pebbles home, instructed to keep them in their pockets and grab hold of them whenever they entered a social situation.

Tip No 46: Circle of excellence
Careful preparation of a person's feelings

Tip No 47: Anchors
Create automatic recall: push the buttons

Staying motivated, looking after yourself, communicating clearly, presenting yourself in an appropriate way and so on may be skills that need to be learnt and practised. They will arise from skills that allow you to move time frames in order to remember why your goal is important and who you believe yourself to be, listen to yourself, feel confident, put yourself in the other person's shoes and so on. All this can be learnt.

What works for Aspies is what works for all us: the biggest difference I can see is that they sometimes require mega-doses. We all profit from structure in our lives: it helps us to know where we are. We all benefit from having people who are on our side: it helps us to feel good about ourselves. We all find value in talking to others: it makes us feel connected.

Tip No 48: Connection
"I like being with you . . ."

In order to work effectively, it is necessary to understand the condition and to create a service built to meet the specific needs of those affected. This is particularly difficult with people who have Asperger's, and in my experience it is not an easy thing to deliver these simple qualities. I am not going to go into an organisational analysis, but I do see that big social care organisations fail to deliver consistent personnel over the necessary time span, and tend to get bogged down in rules and restrictions. I also see that it is hard for mainstream professionals to be as flexible as I think is necessary. Also, all health professionals are in extremely short supply, so it is difficult to get enough time with them when you want it. As I have been arguing, it is also necessary for people in this role to get out of the pathological mindset.

Asperger's is still poorly understood and even more poorly catered for, so the current tendency is for mental health professionals to make the commitment to offer a service, which is a generous and helpful act but overlooks the differences between the two populations. There are some fundamental factors in the conditions and in the expectations of services for people with mental ill health, and people with Asperger's are poorly served by being asked to fit themselves into that particular round hole.

CHAPTER EIGHT

Families are central

F amilies are left holding the baby, and they have to go against the grain of the natural response and make sure that the child always ultimately rules. Coaching the family is a stronger intervention.

Tip No 49: Including family perspectives
What do the others think?

We spring from our families. I was a father at the age of 22, and although I had had no contact with my own father through the course of life, I never stopped to wonder if I knew what to do—I just got on with it. I suspect that we are programmed to be parents, and that children are programmed to teach us. There is a very natural process through childhood and then into adolescence by which we slowly step away from our parents until we are ready to take flight and manage on our own. Again, there are libraries full of books about this process; all I want to do is mention the automatic pattern that happens, and note that there may not be a similar pattern available to a family if their child does not make the move into independence at an appropriate age.

People with Asperger's are often reluctant to fly the nest: things do not work out right somehow, and the default position is to stay at home. The family then moves into unknown territory for which there is no model, no plan. Often this is surrounded by an immediate crisis in the form of depression or anger and conflict, but sometimes it just creeps up—there is never a moment when the motivation is right to pack up and go. Parents find this hard to deal with, usually continuing to do things for the person as though he were still a child, sometimes willingly, sometimes with resentment.

The youngster is also in difficult circumstances, denied the experiences that come to the rest of us automatically once we move into that bedsit. We have to learn to manage money, cook, wash up, do the washing, deal with the hangover and get ourselves to where we are meant to be. The youngster who stays at home is not really in a situation where he can learn to cook or even to manage money: mum and dad do all that and they do it better. It is easier, especially if there is some sort of crisis around, to retire to your room and do things with your computer.

Sometimes things go sour and the family become co-dependent, a kind of warped system in which the problems of one person's behaviour become everyone's problems as they try to save him from himself. This might be around frustration and anger, in which everyone tries to avoid upsetting him despite his increasingly unreasonable hair trigger, or money, in which he gets more than his fair share and uses it selfishly before asking for (and getting) more, or (famously) alcohol or drug abuse and the attendant problems. It may be lower key and just be about him pulling his weight. Often more time and emotional energy than is healthy has to be spent on getting him to make promises which he then breaks. In the end co-dependency is about letting one person control others through fear of his difficult behaviour.

I know a family where the father tells the son, who has finally moved into his own flat, that he can't start to cook unless Dad is there. Dad then finds it hard to make the time to visit, so the new cooker sits unused. I know of a family who used to go out and buy the street drugs for their son on the basis that it was safer for them to do it than for him. I know many families where the son does not handle his money and has never had a bank account of his own, or if he has, he only gets a pocket money allowance—the parents pay all the bills. I know of many families where the son spends all his money on clothes, the pub, friends—the high life—and makes no contribution to the family budget. I am not holding these people up to ridicule in any way; they have found ways that work for them, balancing risks against possibilities, and I know that parents can see risks that we professionals sometimes gloss over in a dangerously haphazard way.

My experience tells me that families become used to the way of living they develop, and are often so afraid of what might happen if they changed anything that they become a factor in the resistance to change which is so characteristic of this condition. It was fashionable a few years ago to suggest (privately, over a cup of tea after a case conference) that maybe Dad was also affected but undiagnosed. This felt a little naughty at the time (and I think it was in fact), but the research is progressing and increasingly suggests that there is a strong heritable strain in the causation of this condition, so there may be something in that. The real reason it was a naughty thing to do was that by implication it disempowers and dismisses the whole family. Whether or not either of the parents has the condition, or some of it, they are still the family and they still need to find a way forward that serves them all.

I think it is clear that your parents' view of you is a powerful factor in your developing view of yourself. I can still hear my mother's voice, though she has been dead for ten years or more, and some of her views on the world, on me and my potential still shine through. Sometimes I recognize my mother in my behaviour and thinking. Sometimes I wish I didn't! Many therapists spend hours working through the patient's relationship with one parent or the other in order for the patient to free her- or himself and take full control of her or his own life. A family living with Asperger's is sometimes faced with an impossible situation, and they do all they can to find a way. Without a map, though, things can turn sour and serve to hold the person back rather than propel him forward.

I am also aware that in default circumstances, when there is no option from the services (which there often is not), the family is the only place a person with Asperger's can go for support. When all else fails, the family is left holding the baby.

This is a situation that families are not programmed to understand, and the strong tendency is to continue to treat the (now adult) young person as though he were still an irresponsible and unstable teenager rather than an adult with the right to control his own life. This becomes a vicious circle, keeping the family stuck, and needs to be replaced with a virtuous circle which supports safe development and appropriate progress.

Tip No 50: Family ecology
Boundaries, consequences, negotiations, space

Tip No 51: Habit implantation
Learning a new habit is not easy—teamwork!

In order to facilitate a move forward, the family has to go against the grain and learn new ways. In this process they need to make sure that the young person with Asperger's has the experience of ruling his own life. This is exceedingly difficult for parents to achieve. They are always mum and dad and the child is always the child, so it is hard to change that communication style. They have almost certainly already tried everything they know and more, and are probably discouraged and frightened of things going wrong. When things do go wrong, the person with Asperger's is far too likely to end up in jail or in the psychiatric hospital, so the dice are loaded.

Tip No 52: Boundaries
Establishing absolutes

Tip No 53: DISC profiling
Learning and personality styles

Yet the voice of the parents is the strongest influence there is, and they can unwittingly undo a lot of the work done by coaching in a moment. In my experience families make their own moves in their own time, not responding well to direction but much better to gentle influence. I conclude, therefore, that coaching the family is the most powerful way forward. Both parents can be supported in developing a team approach, and they can have the satisfaction of completing the task themselves. Once the child has managed to move on (whether to independent or supported life), they are in a position to support this development if they have been fully involved in the work. Also, if they are included in the work, they have to prepare themselves for impending change and sign up to a course of action to create it, so there is less risk of conflict later on.

True independence only comes when you have your own place and you are managing your own economy, your social life and whatever you identify as your needs in a way that is sustainable and low-risk. My son chooses to go off snowboarding, a high-risk activity, but he has health insurance and a reasonable level of skill, and anyway I can't stop him. If he slams into a tree, I will be upset and concerned, but we both know he will be the one who sorts it out.

Of course, independence doesn't mean disconnecting: we are all connected, and families stay close even when the children grow into independence. At some stage the kids stop bringing the washing home, start going to the supermarket like ordinary people, and settle down to a life in which they take all their own decisions—and if they mess it up, they dig themselves out. In my experience this can take them to the end of their twenties, and then, finally, they are truly autonomous.

Every family has its own standards around this process, of course, and different cultures may present a range of different expectations, but generally the process is completed roughly as expected, unless the child has Asperger's syndrome. Of course, some people with Asperger's do move on in the usual time span, but those who don't often come to my attention after a few years because they have ground to a halt in their progress though life, which can be a profoundly depressing experience both for them and for their parents.

Establishing your own independent life is a big factor in developing and bolstering your self-esteem, of course. Returning to Maslow's hierarchy for a moment, it seems we can draw out a social story here.

Once he got himself together and moved into his own flat, Brian enjoyed doing things his own way and looking after his own things and his finances. He made his own choices and felt he was in control of his life. He was proud of his flat, keeping it meticulously tidy. He stayed closely connected to his family and built a circle of friends whom he saw regularly. He felt good about himself for what he was achieving and how he lived his life.

This little story moves up the hierarchy from level two to level four. I don't want to push the model too far, but the point I am making is that independent life is a good thing which can make you feel good about yourself, so long as you still feel safe and connected.

Anthony now lives in his own flat, paying his own rent. He sees his sister most days, and only his family visit him. He is cooking a little, and getting on with his project of recording all his records onto minidisks in preparation for selling them.

Ravi lives in his own flat. His father visits once or twice a week, he goes home to his parents' house three or four times a week, and he will start to cook as soon as his father shows him how to use the cooker. He manages his money, though his father oversees it whenever he wants to.

Jerry has an income from his parents, lives in his own flat, which they bought for him, and takes his washing home for his mother to do. He cooks, but sees very few people.

Families need to be reassured that the risks are acceptable, of course, and there is no better proof than being able to watch things develop into stability. The proof of the pudding is in the eating (another figure of speech, meaning that the best evidence is actually seeing what happens). However, there needs to be space for mistakes and hiccups, because that is how we all learn, and if there is a troubled history, these can create great sensitivity. I remember that when my children were toddlers, we learned not to rush over and make them better if they fell over. If we ran to them, they cried; if we didn't, they picked themselves up, dusted themselves down and started all over again. Sometimes.

Looking out for risks, supporting the person in managing them, staying safe and maintaining an attitude of "can do" rather than "can't do" is demanding for a family which has reasons for anxiety. The outcomes are always uncertain, and the stakes are sometimes very high. Many people with Asperger's are at risk of some sort of breakdown in their twenties as they try to find a way to fly the nest, but if you always do it for them, they don't learn what to do and continue to expect you to rescue them.

It is also undeniable that children outlive their parents. This bereavement usually happens when the child is in their forties or fifties, and if the past forty or fifty years have been spent in the care and under the protection of the ageing parent, the person with Asperger's will be unprepared for the transition. There is nothing new to say on this subject: it is all obvious, but many times the son ends up at home, the family situation going sour, development on hold, and only a crisis can blow it apart enough to allow the possibility of progress. However, progress is so much easier if the person is younger, as his attitudes will be more open to learning and he will not have solidified into dependency.

PART II

ALL ABOUT COACHING

INTRODUCTION

The second part of this book is focused on coaching, a new discipline arising out of a variety of sources, chiefly psychology. I have used my own experience, of course, and have continued to litter the text with tips and stories to illustrate my thoughts.

I have leaned heavily on the school of neuro-linguistic programming (NLP), and my thanks have to go to those who learned with me, and of course those who trained me in this discipline. However, I am a teacher and a parent, and NLP encourages us to create models from an infinity of sources, so I have used these experiences as well as many conversations, training courses, books and conferences. So this is really a summation of everything I know about creating positive change in others. Because the topic is coaching Asperger's, it is a little different from what I might have written if it were about coaching young parents or schoolkids facing examinations. The difference is much more quantitative (there are powerful forces in this syndrome which resist positive change) than qualitative (the same techniques work for all of us; the only differences are in the focus and the strength, and maybe some adaptation to fit the way the syndrome manifests itself). This would be so in any text which brings coaching to a specific group.

Some of this is my own formulation, some of it is lifted directly out the NLP canon, and some of it is borrowed and developed from the library of coaching works that surround me. I hope it will give you the necessary understanding and intellectual titillation to want to explore more and to join the hunt for what works in terms of helping people to move forward.

CHAPTER NINE

Coaching

> "Come to the edge," he said.
> They said: "We are afraid."
> "Come to the edge," he said.
> They came.
> He pushed them . . .
> And they flew.
> Guillaume Apollinaire

Barefoot doctors were established in China as a way of getting healthcare out into the paddy fields, because fully trained doctors would not settle in the countryside. Coaching is a barefoot solution in that it is a pragmatic way of getting a service to people who need something which is not currently in existence or accessible.

These barefoot doctors were community members, still working the paddy fields and fully connected into the community, not part of a separate service. Similarly, coaching is a barefoot solution because coaches are not part of the monolithic health services, but small and flexible and so much more able to adapt to the individual.

This style suits Asperger's much better than any bureaucratic tentacles can. The Chinese doctors were a "can do" solution answering a need in terms of what was possible. Training was brief and scope was narrow, but the contribution was nonetheless valuable. Coaching matches this: it is an epidemic profession nowadays, and there are so many coaches that they are likely to have spare capacity and be accessible. Like barefoot doctoring, coaching is a "can do" response to an epidemic of need.

Although barefoot doctors, being close to the community, were responsible to the community, they could refer on if necessary, so they acted a little like our new NHS walk in centres—easy to get to but not pretending to a high level of specialism. Coaching is a similar solution in that it offers an accessible point of contact which expects people to remain in the mainstream, and if that is not possible it can facilitate a referral to more specialist services. A very useful filtering out occurs, much less divisive and disempowering than joining the waiting list for a referral to the consultant psychiatrist, and of course more efficient in that those filtered out can be saved the journey, leaving more space for those who truly need that level of specialist intervention.

So coaching is accessible and affordable. It is flexible because of the structure—one coach meets the family or the individual and helps them to develop their own way forward to meet their own ambitions. Many other services are shorter term or too brief or infrequent. Coaching, by contrast, aims to be intensive, with contact being weekly or sometimes more frequent, and expects to last a number of months or years in order to create a sustainable difference. And of course it is a cheap solution—coaching is contracted at hourly rates similar to those of other therapists and counsellors.

There is a library of work about coaching: it is as much an epidemic as Asperger's syndrome at the moment. Coaches are rolling off the assembly lines at an unprecedented rate. Of course it is in its infancy as a discipline, and is consequently still under-regulated and very much a free market. There are few recognised agreed standards established yet. However, it comes from respectable sources, there is a long history of coaching both in sporting and in business fields, and there is much more creative space to be explored before the profession becomes set in its ways.

We have already looked in close detail at how the condition manifests itself, and seen how it affects an individual at all levels, many of which are not directly attributable to the organic features of brain architecture and function but are the result of consequent distorted learning arising not only from unusual perception but also from the social experience of growing up in an NT world. It is these consequent features that are open to coaching—how much more effective any of us would be if we escaped our doubts, fears and limiting beliefs about what is possible! Yet coaching, when it comes down to it, is one person structuring a long conversation with another, intending it to be to that second person's benefit. In order to be able to structure that conversation, it is necessary to understand how coaching works so that the coach can be alert to the signs of progress or the reverse. This is the focus of this second part of the book, which I hope will serve to support potential coaches in developing a map for their emerging creative practice.

Coaching, originally mainly for sports and then for business use, is nowadays being developed and applied to "life coaching". This is in tune with the times, of course, the two presuppositions being that the individual is important and infinitely capable and that a diverse and balanced life is desirable (viz. Maslow again). This has arisen out of the humanistic psychology movement and the subsequent growth of the rather less stringently academic personal development movement. Much cynical mud has been slung over the years, and personal development makes a soft target—the hard nuts who sling the mud only have to laugh at the subtle energies that New Agers play with to destroy the sensitivities which are needed to create something positive.

Coaching is primarily about change, which may be internal (acceptance of the situation), external and past-orientated (I was bullied at school and now I think I am odd), or external and future-orientated (I want to get a job). It may also be directed by circumstances (I am homeless because my parents won't let me live with them any more). There is a five point process of change which appears to be universal and which was identified by Elisabeth Kübler-Ross in her work on death and dying. It seems to be relevant for all adaptation to change, and I have found it very helpful to bear in mind and to lead people through to acceptance. The first reaction is denial, in which the subject may suggest that the problem has sorted itself out, may experience a numbness or apathy, and may try to rationalise the problem away. In the second stage he moves to anger, with sabotage, withdrawal and blame placed on the messenger. Thirdly, he goes to bargaining, perhaps offering to cut a deal to save others from harm, or perhaps finding other problems to use the problem-solving energy. The fourth stage is depression, with a feeling of loss of control and perhaps withdrawal, and the fifth and final stage is acceptance, with ownership of the problem and focus on achieving benefits. Whilst I am reminded of many people I have known with Asperger's in all but the final stage, I am also reminded of myself and many other friends and colleagues who have faced changed circumstances. The significance of this lies in the thought that if a person perceives a new situation as being bad news, this is the typical reaction. People with Asperger's syndrome often do not like change in any guise, so this reaction is more likely to find them. The important thing to keep in mind is that this is a normal and healthy process, unless it gets stuck. Coaching can be designed to help people though all five steps, not necessarily in any particular order, but each one important to acknowledge and experience and explore when it comes to call.

Tip No 54: Leading by example
Be the change you want to see

Tip No 55: Naming feelings
Give them words and clarity

The purpose of coaching is to find ways for the subject to discover abilities and energy which were previously hidden, and it consequently leads directly into the unknown. This is a rather high-flown way of saying the obvious, which is that in order to get a new but elusive result, you need to adopt a new method. The process of coaching is to lead the subject to refresh his internal landscape of beliefs, attitudes and self-worth to a point where he will want to learn and practise new skills because he will be more comfortable moving forward than staying stuck. What coaching is not is a personality transplant. The subject is there to find out what he can do himself, not to become someone else. We are born with our personalities, our

motivations and our orientations, and we are born into our circumstances which give us our strengths, our weaknesses and our
interests. The job of a coach is to help the subject to discover his own
best way of getting somewhere that satisfies him.

Tip No 56: Modelling
How do you do that?

Tip No 57: Soundbites and slogans
Tohellwivit!

The precondition for coaching is that the person is free to define
her or his own goals—no one is entitled to impose a world view
on another. The coach's task is to broaden the subject's view of
themselves in their environment so they can find motivation and
purpose in adjusting their way of conducting themselves, and then
to help them keep to their emerging standards as cleanly as possible
so they can experience the full benefit. When the game is on, we
coaches applaud from the sideline, remind people of their own
choices, and offer support when things are tough. What we must
always keep in mind is that the person will have specific values and
beliefs which create their sense of themselves and that they will not
move beyond these. We each have a core of self which we can
recognise as certainty, and new activities and responsibilities need
to fit into this (though it may be possible—indeed, necessary—to
broaden this sense of identity at times).

Tip No 58: Congruence test
I don't know much but I know what I like!

This is a creative approach, and creativity is always vulnerable. Trial
and error necessarily includes error—it is almost impossible to learn
if there is no margin for error—yet errors bring up vulnerabilities
which are sensitive to cynical criticism, and the world is often a
cynical place. Fear is a governing factor here: people are afraid of
what might happen if they try new things, those around them are
afraid of what might go wrong and how bad it might be, and the
professionals are afraid of not knowing what to do. However many

rehearsals one undertakes, the curtain always eventually rises on the first night, and it is the performance that matters, not what has gone before. Failure in rehearsals does not matter, though it can still sting. Coaching hopes to keep the rehearsal as safe and open as possible, so that each failure can be used as a welcome and useful learning point, supporting the person in preparing a better performance for when the time comes.

To a great extent, life coaches are dealing with subjective experience: not questioning a person's ability as much as encouraging them to believe they can do it, to discover feelings that support constructive action. Whilst this is strangely easy for cynics to laugh at, in my view it is also easy to justify. For instance, it is clear that depression, an extreme negative feeling, attacks the will to take action. Similarly, anxiety stops people from trying out new things, and it is very obvious that if you are frustrated with your life, you need to do something new. Some people wake up and jump out of bed with a feeling that they are about to have a good day (remember the last holiday you had?); others wake up dreading the day, knowing it will be another bad one. These are subjective experiences in which your feelings affect what you do. Coaching seeks to help the person find the ability to affect their feelings in order to direct their action.

Every individual has some things they know they will not do as it would go against their sense of themselves (I often notice how children follow their parents in job aspiration, for instance, bankers rarely giving birth to wannabe refuse collectors). Similarly, everyone has some things they expect to do as of right (driving cars, attending university, etc). How this all works is a complicated sociological study; it is enough for our purposes merely to note that it does work. Whilst it is very helpful to recognise that anything can be done if you choose and learn and apply yourself, it is also good to note that some things will be hard for some and easy for others, and that the surrounding family and social systems may well resist unexpected choices. However, things are possible: there are examples of extreme achievement all around us. A blind man climbed Everest, and many run the London Marathon every year, for instance. More prosaically, Nigel Lawson, when Chancellor of the Exchequer in the UK with Margaret Thatcher as Prime Minster, was heroically overweight. He lost the weight, and wrote a book about how he did it. It is each individual's perceptions, feelings and subjective attitude to a task that make the difference, and this is what coaching seeks to affect: change the personal set of feelings, thoughts and sensations woven around a particular objective and you create access to a wider set of resources.

Sports coaches do not expect to break world records themselves but to encourage their protégés to go beyond their own performance and exceed their previous limits. Life coaches do not expect to do things for their clients but to encourage and enable them to do previously unreachable things for themselves. A coach does not have to be exceptionally achievement-orientated, and does not have to be exceptionally talented at the matter in hand—I can teach guitar playing as I am quite good at it myself, but I can coach someone in juggling despite not having the skill myself. What is needed is the ability to help the individual to identify positive goals, recognise their limiting beliefs and attitudes that inhibit them from doing the required work, and find the motivation and resources to do the required work in an efficient and skilful way.

If we are in the midst of the soft revolution of personal relationships and communication now, this new realm of knowledge is being led by positive psychology, neuro-linguistic programming, some other disciplines which may still be considered "alternative" such as NVC (non-violent communication), and many other emerging schools, disciplines and applications. However, as the revolution progresses, many of these will become mainstream areas of study and become more accepted. Currently, these approaches have not attained mainstream acceptance. Freud (and Mesmer before him) fought the same battles before their notions of the unconscious and the structure of the mind became accepted. Psychology and psychiatry have become mainstream disciplines in the past hundred or so years, developing the science of theories and methods and making a vital contribution to our understanding of ourselves. Following this period of growth, it seems that there is now space available to move away from the pathological towards the creative and to bring the spotlight of research to bear on the processes we use naturally to create positive feelings and new strategies. This growth fuels the development of coaching as an application of this enlarging body of scientific work.

In order to understand better how life coaching works, we can pursue the sports coach parallel. Tennis is a game in which you have to develop super-fast reactions, a very precise set of skills, a level of fitness, and a range of attitudinal habits which allow you to recreate repeatedly the necessary state of body and mind to recover from losing a point and rapidly reassert your determination to win the next. A coach will know what is required physically, will have some tricks of the trade and the ability to work with the player to create strong internal processes to develop and maintain the required attitude, and will support the player in developing some personalised rituals and routines that enable him or her rapidly to realign their state without dropping a point.

Timothy Gallwey started something with his book *The Inner Game of Tennis*, which he published in 1974, around the time Richard Bandler and John Grinder started publishing what was to become nuero-linguistic programming, bringing out *The Structure of Magic* and *Patterns of the Hypnotic Techniques of Milton Erickson*. He starts out by suggesting that "every game is played in two parts, an outer game and an inner game". He continues by highlighting the familiar gap between what we want to achieve and our actual performance: "easier to remember than to execute". We would all be satisfied, rich and on permanent holiday if we could successfully think our way forward without hindrance. However, our planning mind chatters on, apparently convinced that a plan conceived is a plan completed. Sometimes it seems that some of my clients believe they can indeed think their way forward, and sometimes I find myself admiring their resultant unfettered audacity and creativity. At other times, however, I can see them slowly lose their belief in their abilities as they find that thoughts and plans do not easily turn into reality for them. Much as we seem to dislike admitting it, this is a way of life for many of us. We face a problem, spend a lot of time thinking about it and make a plan (join Weight Watchers, drink less, get up earlier, exercise), but come February we find that we have not only broken but also forgotten our New Year resolutions. Spring is coming, and we occupy our minds with different problems nowadays, though nothing has changed in our first problem areas because we did not make or follow a step-by-step plan which was both effective and possible.

However, all of us can recognise that on a certain level we already know how to learn new habits and skills without consciously thinking them through—we work unconsciously. We walk, talk, and find our way around a new piece of technology or a new bus route.

In the world of tennis, for instance, racquet technology has allowed service speeds to rise to a level at which you just can't see the ball coming, and yet the returns keep on being made on serves of up to 130 mph.

As the studies widened and people found the ideas helpful and practical, Bandler and Grinder's work led to the appearance of several shelves full of NLP books, most of which are nowadays more about the application of the basic theories than the theories themselves. NLP is a non-prescriptive body of ideas and a way of thinking focused on modelling: discovering how we do what we do so we can hone our techniques and improve our success in getting what we want. The name neuro-linguistic programming contains the fundamental theory: "neuro" refers to how we perceive and encode the information that comes to us though our five senses, "linguistic" is about the influence we exert on ourselves and others though our choice of language, and "programming" holds the idea that we can make adjustments to these processes in order to change the way we do things.

Coaching is not NLP, but NLP has made a significant contribution to coaching and is now one of the prime tools used in the trade. The trade has expanded to include life coaching as a significant part of the industry. I suppose the changes in society over the period between the mid-seventies and the present day have led us to a point where we can more easily accept the idea that individuals can and should learn how to increase their enjoyment of their lives. Along with many others, I signed up for the New Age movement back in the seventies, and became a follower of the new ancient philosophies. Most of us slowly came down to earth and recognised that it takes more than a Hopi ear candle to double your income, whilst the innovators were moving further on, developing ideas which are still coming into focus and general use. Nowadays they are being applied in ever-widening ripples of interesting and diverse areas of influence: management, politics, sport, and occasionally supporting people with Asperger's syndrome. Traditionally, people with Asperger's have been square pegs forced to squeeze painfully into existing round holes for lack of a square template. I hope that society is still developing enough that the cult of the individual can begin to affect the rigidity with which these round holes are maintained—currently it seems to me that the square pegs are unnecessarily and rather cruelly expected to adapt by fitting into these restrictive round holes. I would rather see the people I work with being encouraged to flourish in their diversity.

Coaching is still an open field. This affords us a strong opportunity. Whilst the process of dialogue between academic research and application in practice is still alive and exploratory, it is nevertheless possible to design practice around needs. The coach can use her or his skills and understanding to apply emerging theories to whatever area of development is identified by the client. Life coaching does this to a large extent, but I sometimes find myself in circumstances more unusual than regular life coaches might expect. For instance, I am helping a client write a film script, and am acting much as an editor would. I went to a music gig and a pub with another client, so that he knew how to conduct himself and had some experience up his sleeve for when he meets the desired girlfriend. I have taught people to iron shirts in my time, using the activity to develop thoughts and feelings of personal pride, domestic independence and competence; and I have watched some explicit videos in order to ensure that a client had enough information about sexual practice and experience and that it moved beyond the stereotyped pornographic cartoon. Although these are examples of how this work can become specialist, life coaching is nonetheless the best term for the practice. It is just that many people with Asperger's miss out on the early opportunities that arise to enable learning, and so need coaching in areas others have managed to inhabit naturally.

The essence of coaching is to accept that how you think affects what you do and how you feel because, as we are now learning, these three realms (thought, feeling and action) are interlinked. Science is beginning to accept this in research terms, though practical action seems to be slow in rolling out. Candace Pert is an innovative scientist who has contributed to the birth of the new discipline of psychoneuroimmunology. The new field was first properly recognised in 1984, and her book *Molecules of Emotion* was published thirteen years later. In it she begins to describe the emerging state of knowledge about how the body and mind are linked. This is one of many examples of how the structure of our understanding is shifting: there is now a recognised branch of science called psychoneuroimmunology, and the name tells us of the newly recognised link between the mind, the nervous system and the immune system which inhabit the body. There is a seemingly inbuilt tendency in us to imagine that what we know is complete, only needing a little filling out as research continues, and consequently many people seem unwilling to adapt their thinking radically enough to accommodate new knowledge. Also, to be fair, science necessarily moves slowly, as it is a process of doing the required work to demonstrate the truth behind our assumptions.

Science is now beginning to tell us that our mental and emotional states are interlinked with our health, and to describe that interlinking in detail. However, it seems to me that the world does not yet see how this manifests itself in practice. Children with Asperger's syndrome need a carefully constructed environment to support them in feeling safe and confident so that they are capable of learning. Sensory features of the school environment, such as strip lights that buzz (inaudible to the rest of us), windows that allow visual distraction and the feeling of being observable, background noise, smells from the kitchen, and so on, can all be intolerable to a child with Asperger's. Large group activities such as school assembly, physical activities such as team games (too fast and chaotic), and small group discussions in classrooms can all generate confusion and fear, and of course the social environment, which often features exclusion and bullying, can generate gross discomfort. These features are still rarely adjusted successfully to meet the specific needs of a hypersensitive Asperger's student, and I regularly hear of children who are excluded from school because their behaviour does not suit the school and yet arises from their forced entry into an environment which fails to suit them on so many levels.

The massive unemployment rate of this group is also at least partly attributable to the hostile social and physical environment with which employees are faced. When people fail to fit in for reasons which are primarily to do with their social interaction or their communication styles, or when they find the existing environment hostile, they are disadvantaged; and if their response to these difficulties is to build a method of working which is both idiosyncratic and irritating, and they stick to it no matter how many times they are cajoled to change, this disadvantage can threaten continued employment, no matter if they are good at delivering, or even unusually good at what they do.

Although the situation is improving, and the age of diagnosis is falling, it seems that a person only qualifies for support through exhibiting chronic patterns of unacceptable behaviour. By the time these behaviours are noticed and a response is organised, many years can well have passed, allowing time for the behaviour and the beliefs underpinning it to have become deeply rooted, which of course means that long-term and intense work is then required to support the person in moving forward.

I heard a story recently which helps to illustrate the special strength of coaching. Foxes are rife in London, and my friend met someone who is dedicated to managing this problem rather than eradicating it. He likes wildlife, but recognises that some people dislike foxes living in their garden. Rather than hunting them, poisoning them or destroying their dens, he creates a hostile environment so that they freely wander off to find somewhere else to live. So, for instance, as they are creatures which like predictability, he changes the smells and sounds around on a daily basis. Like any family which likes peace and quiet and has freedom of choice, they move house. People with Asperger's are often faced with this sort of hostile environment, but they are denied the freedom to choose, and are forced to exist in an environment which gives them stress, anxiety and discomfort. We know from Candace Pert and others that this results in unhealthy blood chemistry, which itself can create negative thinking. Conversely, we know that part of the equation to produce positive thinking and creative action is to produce blood chemistry which supports optimism, motivation and proactive attitudes.

It is often not possible to change the external environment, and the person has to learn to deal with adversity. There is a triangulation which is fundamental to coaching: behaviour, internal state and cognition all affect one another interactively. Make a change with any one of these and the others will respond. Regular exercisers know that they feel different after the run. Irregular eaters know that a good meal can change how they feel. Regular meditation changes your brain patterns and blood chemistry. People who think strangers are looking at them tend to feel uncomfortable in crowds; yet some disabled or disfigured people seem to manage (Alison Lapper and Simon Weston come to mind). Thoughts both germinate and arise from beliefs, and what you believe generates your instinctual responses to situations. It is these instinctual responses, arising from the unconscious mind, that prevent us from keeping our New Year resolutions. Our minds also do a lot of semi-audible thinking, telling each of us what to think; strangely, in humans this seems naturally to be much more negative than positive. Affirmations were popular in my New Age days: they are present-tense statements of how one is on the road to enlightenment, prosperity and perfection ("I am filled with power, strength and beauty", and so on), as was mind training ("Every day in every way I get more and more . . ."). Someone pointed out recently that we give ourselves affirmations all the time, not noticing that they are mostly negative. Affirmations are designed to affirm your new beliefs, but they often serve to affirm old, negative and outdated beliefs you formed at some sensitive age of childhood and adolescence ("You stupid halfwit!" or "Fat cow, you can never say no to ice cream, can you?"). We hardly hear our self-talk, but it is insidious, often dwelling much more on our failings and perceived weaknesses than our successes and strengths. It is the beliefs we hold which generate this self-talk and keep us stuck painfully in the old familiar muddy round hole.

Behaviour is generated by thoughts and feelings, which arise from an individual's inner state, which in turn is created by the global processing of the mind and body. We have already explored how this global processing can be described in terms of the Triad of Impairments as arising from systemic differences in brain and body function, which may arise from genetic causes. The thoughts and feelings often associated with Asperger's are ones of frustration, loneliness, isolation, difference, self-consciousness and dependence. These patterns change with age, of course, and the people I know are also capable of excitement, pleasure, humour, sadness, laughter, and so on. It is the negative and persistent thoughts and feelings that can create long-term damage, though, and those who are unlucky and are left with these patterns can fall into a vicious circle in which their internal negativity produces behaviour which has the effect of reinforcing the negative beliefs as people distance themselves or try to control them. Ultimately this leads to the creation of behaviours which attract the attention of the services and can eventually result in a diagnosis. These behaviours will include anger, frustration and possibly violence. People can also become depressed (I am told that the suicide rate for people with Asperger's syndrome is noticeably higher than the national average). Powerlessness can set in, which leads to dependence and resistance to responsibility. People spend their time in safe but isolating activities such as computers, music, TV, running and swimming, all of which are solitary activities which can offer respite from a mind running a negative and endless thought pattern. In addition, people developing problem behaviours may be uncaring or unaware of other people, talk to the point of boredom in others, or control and frustrate those around them so that new relationships do not develop and the person becomes increasingly isolated. At an extreme level, this can develop to a point where the person will not go out, or even come down from his bedroom.

Beliefs are strong, and they give us the coherence of personality which is so fundamental to humanity. However, they can also limit us at times. Unless we shift a belief pattern, any behavioural change will be stressful and likely to revert—think of the weight loss industry, or the class system that keeps Britain so great. The key to long-term and lasting change is to create a change in a person's belief system. When working with people who have Asperger's, it is often also necessary to create belief changes in the family, which has developed a way of protecting and retaining the person as the condition unfolded itself over the years. Change the beliefs and you change behaviour, but the converse is not always true. However, if you enter the triangulation and create change in any of the three elements (behaviour, internal state, cognition), you then have space to make use of coaching skills to encourage positive change in beliefs. The one thing you can be sure of in this is that you can see behaviour, though it is a considerable skill to develop awareness of micro-behaviour (breathing pattern, eye movement, gesture).

When you assume that all behaviour gives the highest quality information, reflecting both conscious and unconscious processes, you realise that you have found the doorway into effective change. When you further realise that we are all continually and unavoidably engaged in a highly responsive behavioural dance, this begins to introduce you to the core of coaching. My behaviour as a coach responds to the client's behaviour, and this creates rapport and trust, opening doors. I use this to help the client to check that his goals are truly things to be accepted and welcomed, and to define his personal best route to them. I use my behaviour and my perception of the client's behaviour to steer him towards an experience of the most powerful set of resources (thoughts, feelings, memories, states of body and mind) so that he can begin to create a "future memory" of success: powerful, believable and multi-sensory. This composite representation of the future is stored as an interesting and exciting attractor which he will recognise as he moves towards his goals.

When you believe that you always get tongue-tied at parties, you avoid talking to people and have a miserable time, relegated to the kitchen, sinking into a cheap red wine stupor as your self-talk runs rampant in your head and you notice that everyone else is having a great time. Conversely, if you come to believe that you can always find a way round a difficulty, you launch fearlessly into the chitchat round. At 15 or 16 I was a shy young man. It is hard to believe now, and I launch many of my clients into a state of disbelief if I start with that statement, but it is true. I had never met girls really—single-sex schools and a rather isolated family made sure of that, and I was fearlessly committed to underachievement (a way of proving all my negative affirmations). I was also over six feet tall, as thin as a cheap chopstick, clumsy and non-sporty, and so very vulnerable to the confident putdown. I consequently hated parties, though the attraction of the girls and the cheap red wine was too strong to stop me going. After a few red-faced, tongue-tied moments, I discovered the trick: bounce every question straight back and get the other person to talk about themselves. It was a revelation to me, and I lived (enigmatically) on this trick for years as I wandered off into my early twenties. I no longer hated parties and rapidly learned how to be witty and amusing, started to read about Oscar Wilde and Noel Coward, and having eventually thrown myself in, learned to swim in the social pond.

Coaching seeks to intercede in the essentially negative processes which keep us caught in negative and recurring patterns, so that we can amend our beliefs to allow new behaviour to arise which will bring us to a new situation in our life. We sabotage vicious circles which lead downwards and install virtuous ones which lead us into situations where we develop further and further again.

Specifically, coaching Asperger's is sometimes assisted by the presence of a mind which is vulnerable to thought viruses. I remember Mike, who was easily open to influence in this way. His mother reported that if he spent a day with his paranoid and delusional friend, he came away from that experience to all intents and purposes psychotic. When he spent time with me, however, he came away feeling more powerful and hopeful, because I spent time giving him thoughts about how things might start to work in his favour and about his essential qualities.

Tip No 59: Installing thought viruses
Tell him good things about himself—give him a gift

CHAPTER TEN

Practical coaching

C oaching feels to me like a spiral process: you keep on revisiting the same old patterns but from continually changing perspectives. The hope is that the coach can use her or his skills to extend the spiral so upward progress can be made faster and further than would otherwise be the case. The fundamentals I will describe shortly are important to work with and to keep fully in mind as you bravely go. The coach will use a variety of coaching skills in order to make sure these fundamentals are still actively in play as the plan unfolds. The processes form the basis of a coaching plan, and in practice (never as simple as theory!) the coach's job is to keep the subject aware of all this while taking new steps. You learn by doing. However, progress can understandably be slow if the person is working against a backlog of negative experiences.

The first step in being coached, therefore, is to recognise a few fundamental thoughts and to explore thoroughly how these thoughts affect your understanding of the way you lead your life. These five thoughts are designed sequentially to open the mind to acceptance of the coaching process:

1. You are responsible
2. You need a new way

3. You need a personal plan
4. You have to learn as you go along
5. Don't kid yourself

Then you can begin to move forward, and as you do, there are some processes to follow, again sequentially designed:

1. Acceptance
2. Ownership
3. Choice
4. Learning
5. Practice
6. Planning
7. Criticism
8. Commitment
9. Adherence
10. Review
11. Adjustment
12. Perseverance

The coaching tips I offer will create a mixed response: some will make sense and be directly applicable while others may well remain obscure or not feel right in one way or another. Often they feel banal and obvious, which is understandable, though my observation tells me that people are often not as good at using these banal and obvious points as they think they are. I see others failing to do so, and yet I notice that people often mention how easy I am to talk with, how friendly, how nice! Which is all true of course: although I am using a studied art to achieve this, I also have to mean it and to act on my image, or I will very soon have no friends. The point of all this is to highlight that we are using natural and banal processes, but in a more aware and focused way, to support people in making the natural journey towards their own idiosyncratic maximum effectiveness so that the progress they make can be enjoyed and maintained.

I use these techniques on a daily basis and they make sense to me; I have made choices from within the NLP canon as well as education, parenting, and my own personal experience. Techniques are useful if you feel comfortable with them. Different people will respond differently to suggestions according to their circumstances, knowledge and personality, and coaching subjects will all require different sets of techniques to suit their specific orientations. What matters is that the coach understands that the person will only take up new possibilities which feel right at the time, and that beliefs drive behaviour.

Coaching thinking structure

My coaching is informed by my experience at work, of course, and my own learning, primarily in education, counselling and NLP. In order for me to support someone in moving forward (and all my clients want this as they are all frustrated in one way or another), it is first necessary for him to be clear in his own mind that it is possible and desirable. Stage one, then, is opening his mind to the value of stepping out into unknown territory.

I have developed this series of thoughts which will support that process. On the one hand it is helpful to begin with fundamentals—they are non-threatening and help understanding. On the other hand, without an acceptance of these fundamental points, progress will not be possible or sustainable. They are also sequential in that there is an internal logic connecting the argument together, which builds from one point to the next. However, the thoughts are not the techniques, though these arise from the thoughts. Rather they serve to open the mind to the possibility of using techniques, so they are an essential place to start as they generate a willingness to use the techniques.

Tip No 60: Consequences
If this, then that: night follows day, and the rule is the rule

Bertrand Russell said: "Nothing is so exhausting as indecision, and nothing is so futile." Coaching moves beyond the usual half level of commitment to the discovery of your potential by challenging your perceived limitations in order to find out what is really possible.

1. You are responsible

When you understand that you are responsible for the outcome of your communication (or perhaps you might realise that the meaning of your communication is the response it gets), you come back to being in control of your life in a powerful way. When you know you can choose how to feel, you also have to acknowledge that you are choosing how you respond to circumstances. A situation is not in itself stressful; you choose to experience it as such. No one can make you sad or angry; you choose to feel that way. Coaching can also be seen simply as the process of enabling the subject to understand this so he or she can learn the skills of self-management.

Self-management begins with the understanding that the body is a system connected internally and externally. A system is defined as a collection of bits which together create something, and which rely on each other. Think of a car, with the engine, the brakes, the steering and the driver. In the case of a human, the nervous system can be split (over-simply) into conscious, automatic and unconscious. I often ask people who they think is driving their bus. If the conscious mind were truly in charge, they would have arrived at their destination of choice by now (happy, wealthy, fit, tanned). In fact, there is an uneasy compromise stuck between the thinking mind and the unconscious one where the doubts and fears and limitations exist. This mind, however, is directed to an extent by the peptides in our blood. Some of these will come from the food we eat, and we can adjust the cocktail by (for instance) exercising, changing our diet, and even choosing what films we watch, what books we read and what stories we tell ourselves. We are electrochemical beings in fact, although as science has developed we have learnt to think that the neurons and synapses run themselves in isolated splendour. It is not so: they are affected directly by the chemical conversation which also goes on in our bodies. Electricity is an essentially chemical reaction. One of the main functions of coaching is to interfere with established patterns at this level. By adopting new behaviour and thinking habits, you can affect how you feel, and therefore how you behave.

We are connected internally. The catchphrase has become "mind-body-spirit", and the most functional explanation I have found about spirituality is that it is recognisable by a feeling of connectedness. No man is an island: our actions impinge on others, and we are all born into families, which act as our mainstay for better and for worse. More than that, it is hard (or impossible) to get something done all alone. We are also connected externally. If my editor was not hounding me, I would be less likely to write this book, and if I had not got a promise to publish, I might feel as though I was wasting my time, which would make the final full stop even less likely to emerge. Your actions have consequences, and when you take responsibility for this you become more powerful, as it is then possible to enlist others in your journey.

This may sound grandiose, and can be: grand actions come from grand plans and happen through the concerted energy of a team. Starting a business or a project will necessarily include other people, and if they believe in what you are doing and want it to happen, you have a meeting of minds and a synergy which gives you more energy together than any of you would have alone. On a more prosaic level, if you meet someone and fancy her, the courting process can be seen as one of enrolling her in your life and becoming enrolled in hers. When two people believe in each other, the conditions for intimacy arise. A client of mine wants to move to an ex-Iron Curtain country because he is disgusted with the lack of morality and the development of the surveillance society here. He is connected to the society he lives in, even if he does not welcome this fact, and he has a rather grandiose emigration plan to fall back on.

The ultimate thought arising from all this is that you have sole responsibility for how you experience your life and for how your actions impact on others. All your actions have some effect on others, as those of others do on you. Your actions arise from your own thoughts and feelings, which in turn arise from the electrochemical flow in your body. Coaching has to focus on finding a way for the client to manage that electrochemical conversation to the best ends. If you recognise that you are responsible for the effects of all your communications (verbal and non-verbal, internal and external), you recognise the importance of learning how to manage yourself. It is the communications that form the connections. Recognition of the neuro-linguistic connections gives you an entry point to managing the programming.

2. You need a new way

As soon as you recognise that you are responsible for the effects of all you do, it becomes clear that you need a new way. You are responsible for the effects of your actions. You want something to happen. You have yet to achieve that goal. You need a new way. These are only baby steps really, but as Timothy Gallwey asks, "Why does it take so long to break an old habit and learn a new one?" We are reliant on our habits, and the internal connections which create them are multilayered enough to be powerful and resilient to change. It is easy to do something different once, but much more of a challenge to maintain that change. Smokers sometimes "give up" smoking several times in a year. Old habits die hard, especially if the unconscious mechanisms are not addressed. The baby step of recognising that you need to find a new way is worth bringing to the spotlight in all events, and if the person with Asperger's is particularly resistant to change, it becomes even more important.

It is obvious that someone who is dissatisfied needs to do something different. However, from my own experience of people with and without Asperger's, I know that it is exceedingly familiar territory to get stuck with a belief that says "I must do the same thing again, but harder". Sometimes, of course, this is true—consistency and application are very necessary in order to achieve something, and to some extent, following a strategy harder and for longer than is usual is in fact doing something different. The skilful ones amongst us, though, are those who think about the design of their strategy, and include consideration of the unconscious, emotional and feeling realms as well as the activities involved. I know several people with Asperger's, however, who cannot get beyond thinking that all you have to do to get a girlfriend is say hello to a nice looking woman. My view is that you need to have things to talk about; you need to be fairly good at finding out what interests her and be able to make her laugh and feel safe with you. I also think (just from my own personal list of abject failures) that you are much more likely to succeed if you already know someone than if you are cold-calling. There are a lot of considerations here, but the essence is that if what you are doing is not bringing you the results you want, you should try something different.

On a different level, it is sometimes hard to accept that you have previously tried and failed: it is unpleasant to acknowledge that fact. However, when you do, you may find that you are more open to either changing your goal or changing your strategy. Failure is a strange concept: whilst it may be objectively true that something does not happen, it is your choice whether to process this as failure or useful information to be used next time. This "reframing" is a way to open doors. Allowing yourself to perceive failure closes them.

Inherent in this, of course is the notion that you want something. Wanting is an amazingly normal human experience—it seems as if we are built, or at least taught from a very early age, to be dissatisfied. Wanting can be highly motivating, so dwelling at length on something you want and describing it to yourself can create strong motivation. Obviously, if you don't want anything, there is no need for coaching. However, it is often very difficult to see what you really want because of the wealth of fantasy the human mind can create. The process of coaching can sometimes be one of encouraging people to chase what they think they want so they can discover if something more down-to-earth is actually a more satisfying ambition. Constant review is a vital part of learning: it supports consistency and saves the energy that can be spent chasing rainbows. However, wanting something is not always external or material; sometimes a feeling of confidence or connectedness, or perhaps relaxation, is prize enough.

Then we have to consider how strange the human mind is in its operation: it tells you on a very regular basis (and volubly in my case) what you need to do and how you should run the country and redesign cities. Although we all (I hope!) have these thoughts, as well as a continuous flow of get-rich-quick schemes and weight loss plans, nothing much happens often. Somehow thought does not easily change to action. This is either because the thoughts are faulty or because the motivation is weak, I suppose. Coaching takes care of the motivation, of course, so it may be useful to consider that whatever the new solution is, those which are going to work will probably not feel logical—if you could have thought your way forward, you would have, so something new is required, and its newness alone will create some odd sensations.

It is likely in fact that a new course of action will feel unfamiliar, unwelcome, unimportant and uncomfortable. We all get stuck in our ways, and people with Asperger's seem to do so more than the rest of us. Often this is because of fear of change and fear of the unfamiliar, and it is absolutely necessary that the person being coached is willing to undergo the uncomfortable experience of trying something new without being completely sure about it.

3. You need a personal plan

Going forward without a plan is reckless if you are in the jungle (or even if you are in London, come to think of it). A plan gives you a way to know if you are progressing or not. It is a fact of life that people are ill-disciplined. Those who are disciplined are sometimes labelled disapprovingly as "control freaks". In order to make the most of coaching and do the best you can to make sure you are moving forward, you need some sort of a plan. Ideally a plan for change incorporates all sorts of elements that will keep you fired up, motivated and committed, although in practice it may be better to make the simplest plan possible, just focusing on the critical path of major stepping stones. What really matters is that the plan is something to which no part of you objects. Single-mindedness is stronger than being in two minds.

A plan reassures you that you are moving forward and gives you occasion to celebrate as you go, which is a good thing to do. It also allows you to predict when difficult times are coming, and it allows you to note exactly when (or if) you want to give up, so giving you information about what you need to address in order to have another go. Of course a good plan makes sure you don't overlook things (to-do lists are great: you don't have to remember what comes next if you have it written down).

People with Asperger's are notorious for finding it difficult to generate strategies which are, in effect, a middle term plan. It is often easier to see what needs to be done today and what you finally want than it is to see the path from here to there, each step new and uncomfortable. So a really good plan needs to be almost impossible to avoid and extremely attractive to follow. It also takes into account the things you tend to overlook in the heat of the moment.

Tip No 61: Time frames (short, mid, long)
You have to make a move into the mid term in order to make change happen

3. You have to learn as you go along

However, if you could think your way forward, you would have done by now. Too much rigid planning makes it very likely that you will experience failure at some point, and this can stop you in your tracks. If you know in advance that part of the plan is to explore what is possible and to adjust your plan in the light of experience, then any perceived failure becomes an opportunity to become even smarter as you find more effective ways around problems and obstacles.

Another way of looking at this is to recognise that you will sabotage yourself. This is just another way of saying that a new way is required: old ways have been proven to be ineffective. We all seem to have mixed motivations and to get in our own way really easily. Better to realise this at the outset and consider how to set the saboteur at peace than to be disheartened when it happens. It is useful to spend a while considering the downside of change, and to make sure that your plan manages any losses in an acceptable way sometimes eating chocolate is nice! And pizza.

And of course you don't have to do anything you don't want to: you are perfectly entitled to change your mind as you go along and to alter either your goal or your strategy. It is much better to feel free and autonomous than to feel trapped, although it is also useful to notice if you do keep on changing course and how often you do it, so that you help all parts of yourself come to terms with what you really are prepared to work towards.

4. Don't kid yourself

The successful journey will not be as you imagine it to be. It is essentially a journey into the unknown. Who would guess how uncomfortable it could feel to be with a new lover? Who would predict that getting a job would be so difficult for some people to achieve? Who would have predicted that an employment agency would ask one client for his passport, or that he would not be prepared to show it? There will be unexpected highs and lows as you break out of familiar territory. In all probability, whatever goal you set yourself, the moment of reaching it will not be as you imagine.

However, until you have tried everything anyone has ever thought of, you cannot say that achievement of a particular goal is impossible, only that you find it hard to get there. Whether or not you get where you want to be, and whether or not you enjoy the process, you will learn about your own capabilities, which in itself is valuable. As you develop your life and incorporate the techniques of change, you will become more accurate, but the journey (long and winding) is at least as important as the brief moment of arriving.

An example will be helpful at this point. Imagine Catherine, a young woman with Asperger's, aged 19. She wants to travel, but is afraid of being alone, of the risk, of being confused, and of not enjoying the foreign experience. She is not sure how to use airports, speaks no foreign languages, but wants to see the world before settling down to a university course. Her parents are against the idea, afraid that she will be lost, exploited, attacked, confused and unable to manage. She is prone to anxiety and resultant stress.

First she can realise that because she is connected internally she may be able to manage and control the stress. She could also examine her motivation and consider whether it is true that she wants to travel, and if she does, whether she really wants to go as far as she was planning: maybe a trip to France or Spain would be enough for her. It may be that her desire to travel is fuelled by a desire to run away, or to have one last fling at doing what other people do before settling down at college, or to prove something to herself or her family. Any of these motivations may be fine, but many of them could be met in other ways. She may have only half realised her dream, and it may be that she also wants to write about her travels, make some money and get some recognition. If that is so, perhaps she needs to start contacting features editors and attempt to secure a publishing deal.

However, she is also connected externally, principally to her parents, and she does not want to have a conflict with them. In fact it may be useful for her to listen to their view of her and to consider what to do about their fears. When she does this, she could start to make plans which are informed by the fears. How is she going to get along without speaking any foreign languages? Should she find a travelling companion? Start to learn fast? Or do what most people do and muddle by in English whilst picking up the local language?

Recognising her connectedness, she makes whatever adjustments are necessary to make sure she is fulfilled by the experience, but also that she is safe. She listens to her parents; she does not seek conflict with them and recognises that they may have a useful perspective. She does not want to make big mistakes and stumble into a crisis.

So part of her new way is to work with her family. She may need to learn at least some foreign phrases and go into some cafés to practise, or even sign up for an intensive language course, and start to meet strangers and develop her skills in dealing with them in order to be sure she has the necessary ability. She certainly needs to sharpen up on her budgeting skills and her mental maths around exchange rates and the cost of things in shops. Her motivation is partly to have something to talk about when she gets to university, so she needs to start a diary habit, though of course, being modern, she will choose to start a blog. She needs to get a short-term job to pay for at least part of her trip, and as she hates getting up and meeting people, this is difficult for her every day; but she gets used to it, as you do. In fact she has a lot of fear about the loneliness of her plans, but she doesn't want to be thrown together with another person because she thinks they would not get on. She recognises her fear and talks to her parents about it; they are relieved to hear her talk about her feelings. She also talks to them about sex, so they know she is safe and prepared, should she find a holiday romance. She begins to make concrete plans, choosing where to go and sketching out her itinerary. She blogs it, so her parents and friends can read it, and begins to search for a publisher because she wants to tell her story and be noticed. An editor is interested, but wants her to go to the USA rather than South East Asia; she refuses to do this until she thinks it through and learns about the geography of the USA, and realises that she can include the Caribbean and go to South America afterwards under her own steam for a couple of weeks. She is excited, and her parents have to talk to her firmly about the job and the need to make a written plan of all the things she has to do in preparation, in order to achieve this trip safely. She finds out that travelling takes a lot of organising and boring things.

Tip No 62: Developing family responsibility
Other points of view—how can you support the changes going on? What do you fear?

She makes a five-step plan:

1. Decide on areas to visit and check out what to do there.
2. Earn enough money.
3. Make bookings.
4. Finalise and agree the publication of her blog.
5. Pack from a planned packing list.

She also agrees to take emergency phone numbers of a few contacts her family can rustle up.

Her parents persuade her to make fallback and emergency plans, and to build in quiet safe times to keep her stress manageable. She becomes ill and loses a week's earnings, and decides she has to borrow the necessary money in order to keep to her publishing schedule, so she takes out a bank loan against the income from writing.

She considers why she fell ill, and realises that it was because of her mounting stress. She considers abandoning the whole trip, but realises that all she needs to do is limit her planning to the weekend, when she is not working, and that she needs a lot of downtime watching the TV in order to manage the rising excitement. She begins to learn to monitor her stress levels and take breaks in advance of actually becoming ill.

When the time comes to go, she is sick and miserable, and she hates the long flight to LA. When she gets there, she is frightened and spends an hour in the airport before she can find the courage to go and find a taxi. Later, in her hotel room, having been unable to eat, she writes this up in her blog, calls her parents, and goes to sleep, miserable. When she wakes up in the early afternoon of the next day, she reads over the story she wrote for herself about her trip, and is reminded that she made all this happen herself because she wanted it so badly. She picks up the phone and calls her mother's friend, who lives in Santa Monica, and is invited out for lunch. At lunch the friend introduces her to some kids of her own age who invite her to go out into the hills the next day . . .

CHAPTER ELEVEN

Coaching process

S o, having prepared your mind for action, there is a process to follow in addressing your desire to move forward:

1. Acceptance
2. Ownership
3. Choice
4. Learning
5. Practice
6. Planning
7. Criticism
8. Commitment
9. Adherence
10. Review
11. Adjustment
12. Perseverance

1. Acceptance

The past is what it was, the present is what it is. You have so much money, so many debts, so many friends, possessions and so on. Good and bad things have happened to you, and nothing can be undone now. You are prone to this or that sort of thinking and feeling and your body is too fat or too thin or too tall or too small.

In all this you can separate the facts from the feelings and the feelings from the thoughts. The fact is that I weigh whatever I weigh and my body mass index is at exactly that point. My feelings about this might include sadness, disappointment and anger, and my opinion about it might be that I am over the hill and too weak to try and change things.

Once I have accepted all this, I am freer to move forward to the next stage. Without accepting it, my feelings are more likely to undercut me than to support me, and my opinion, hidden in the recesses of my soul, could sap my energy. A clear-sighted look at what is really going on in myself can lead me to accept that it will take real effort, physical, mental and emotional, to move me to a place of commitment to lose weight and follow whatever programme I choose to use.

"Here I am, overweight by two and a half stones, at the line between overweight and obese. I am embarrassed, annoyed and disappointed, and I have almost given up believing, or even caring, that it could be different. Too old now." My blood chemistry changes from the stress of denial to a cocktail of embarrassment, annoyance and disappointment.

2. Ownership

All these facts, opinions and feelings are mine, and I have control over my life and experience, although I am connected to others I want to take care of. I am who I am; my story is mine and has created the person I am today, busy writing the next page of my history. In truth I do want to change something, and so there is a gap between what I am and what I want to be.

"So those are the facts. Here is how I feel about them, and this is what I currently think about it all. I do want to change this in order to feel energetic and good about myself again, so I had better generate a plan." My blood chemistry changes again as I prepare to pick myself up, dust myself down . . .

3. Choice

If you allow yourself a moment to really make an informed choice about moving forward, this is a motivating moment. There is no compulsion in life, only consequences, and you can choose to have whatever consequences are available.

Losing weight requires a change in eating, sleeping and exercise habits, and some difficult internal changes in how you feel about yourself. Getting a girlfriend requires that you adjust your behaviour quite considerably, and then you have to adapt your life to meet her at some point.

Every gain involves a loss, and the more you dwell on these losses, the more likely it is that you will truly commit to the change you really want. The moment you truly commit to something is an important one to pass through: it is a good time to check your doubts and fears and your willingness to take on the task.

"So here is the plan. It involves always leaving some food on my plate and paying really good attention to the process of eating—I can't read while I am eating any more, nor watch T.V. The plan requires that I always decide what I want to eat when I am hungry, so my shopping habits will have to change. Hmmm. So I will do it, and I will give myself three months to see what is possible." More change as I become single-minded.

4. Learning

Sometimes the necessary skills are obvious: it may be necessary to undertake some study and pass exams in order to get a job or a place at university, for instance, or it might be important to learn to drive. However, the necessary skills may be more personal, such as getting up earlier, doing the housework, or domestic tasks which are not intrinsically difficult but sometimes seem very unwelcome.

The skills which are more often overlooked, though, are the soft skills of managing your own state so that you can create the progress you want. This can include obvious and necessary things such as anger management, but also (returning to positive psychology) creating and maintaining motivation, optimism and energy, and managing stress, tiredness, anxiety and other limiting factors.

"OK, so I will get a hypnosis CD. I will listen to it at least once a week, and leave the book on the table. I will tell everyone what I am doing, and I will spend the first week always eating alone, without reading, so I can practise that awareness thing. I will keep a diary so I can keep a check on how I am feeling, and will arrange to talk to a friend every week specifically about what I am doing."

5. Practice

It always seems logical to practise new skills until you are confident. One of my clients has arrived at a stage where he is confident that he can rescue himself from his deep-seated anxiety and social phobia. Because he has become confident, he is now able to address questions around his future plans without giving in to doubts about his ability to cope: he knows that he can handle himself in difficult situations, and he knows exactly what he has to do in order to achieve this. His posture, breathing and religious beliefs all play a part in this, as do his choice of thoughts and self-talk. He has practised these in the street, in short adult education courses, and in a variety of new experiences he has given himself, and he is now working on formulating a plan for the future which uses his new-found confidence. At the time it felt as though he was following his plan. As he moves forward, though, his plan is enlarging.

"OK, I know what I am doing: maybe I need to give myself a few days when I am relaxed and not busy, so I can get used to how it all works. I am using different shops at different times, and cooking less, and suddenly I like cooking rice again. I'll start properly after a week of messing about to see what it feels like."

6. Planning

The better the plan, the more chance you have of success. A route map can give you milestones, awareness of the risks, the skills you need, supplies and emergency plans, short cuts, pit stops, companions and fail-safe mechanisms. Maybe it should be written, or maybe it is enough to carry it in your head. My weight loss example is very simple in essence: eat with awareness, always leave a little, talk to a friend once a week, and keep a diary; stop to see what is happening at three months. Make a note in the diary!

7. Criticism

Do an "idiot check" internally and externally: make sure the plan is as good as it can be and the ambition is sound. Just stand back and consider what you may have overlooked, blocked out or forgotten. In my plan, if I find myself stuffing on ice cream, all I have to do is to listen to the CD again and start the habits again, having taken the time to work out why the ice cream fairy came to call: Stress? Tired? Emotionally battered? How can I manage that moment better next time?

8. Commitment

Choose to make it happen.

"OK, finally I have done all I can do. Do I want to go through with this or not?" It really is acceptable to turn the whole plan down, though there are consequences to that decision. At this point, having worked though in detail the implications and cost of the plan, it may be a very sensible thing to turn your back on the whole enterprise and decide to leave it. If you do that, then there will be no regrets: "I looked at the whole prospect and decided I didn't want to do it. There was not enough benefit to outweigh the loss."

> Until one is committed, there is hesitancy, the chance to draw back, always ineffectiveness . . . Whatever you can do or dream you can, begin it. Boldness has genius, power and magic in it. Begin it now. [Goethe]

9. Adherence

Having spent the time planning, it is only fair to yourself to remember to follow the plan, constantly reviewing, until you get to where you want to be. Change is not always very attractive, especially to Aspies, and sometimes it may be useful to be reminded that it is in fact an essential part of getting new goals.

10. Review

Stop and review, but not until you have established the new habit. At the end of about three months, think about whether to go on, stop, or change the plan. Many people seem to unconsciously choose to keep on doing something, notwithstanding that it does not lead to the desired effect, so you need to stop and make a conscious choice.

11. Adjustment

Amend the plan in the light of your experience and the best views of those around you.

12. Perseverance

It may seem obvious, but recall the New Year resolutions. It is so easy to get caught up in a different plan before you have exhausted all the possibilities of the current one. Napoleon reminds us that "victory belongs to the most persevering", while that well-known dyslexic Winston Churchill repeatedly said: "Never give in. Never give in. Never give in."

CHAPTER TWELVE

Boundaries and behaviour

"God, give me grace to accept with serenity the things
that cannot be changed, courage to change the things that
should be changed, and the wisdom to distinguish the one
from the other."

Reinhold Niebuhr

I want to take a short section to outline a behavioural approach
and consider how it can be used in a family and coaching context,
with adults or children, and to make some reference also to other
structures such as assertiveness.

Some feel that the behaviourist approach reduces humanity to
the level of animals. Part of me thinks this is fair; and part of me
thinks there are more forces at work within us which raise us in some
way beyond the natural dignity of the animal kingdom, but also
complicate the issue. I would not be writing this book if I had not
been introduced to this approach when I was a teacher; I would be
in some other area of work altogether. I have no idea what the alternative future for me would have been, but without being introduced
to this approach, I would have got out of teaching altogether. I was

teaching half a dozen autistic children and they were destroying my vision of what was possible—I could not find a way to get their attention. The lesson I was given then remains as fresh now as it was then. It opens the door to a more positive relationship which in turn opens the door to more complicated and NT-friendly ways of being. I want to share it: a refreshingly well controlled and crisp approach which may be a good antidote to all the confusing interactivity of coaching, and a wonderfully effective crisis intervention which allows you to develop a whole new way of relating. There is a wealth of experience and evidence that a behaviourist approach is most likely to achieve rapid results in changed behaviour, but it is not always clear how this can be organised in the context of a family, especially if the subject is adult.

Behaviourism suggests that we all work for rewards. When an individual exhibits some unwanted behaviour, the suggestion is that the behaviour brings a reward, which can be identified purely by observing what happens next. In essence, all that is needed is to adjust things so that the reward arrives immediately after a desirable piece of behaviour.

Ah, if it were that easy . . .

First of all, behaviour does not seem to come in small packages: my pupils used to spit, kick and punch at the same time as they spilled a drink, so you have to discipline yourself to identify specific and discrete pieces of behaviour with start and finish points that differentiate them from all the other pieces of behaviour in the patterned chain of interaction.

With older people, of course, there is the notion that as they grow, they earn the increasing right to choose how they lead their lives. This is only true if they are responsible and interactive: it is not acceptable for people to tread on other people's feelings, and it is expected that we do not abuse each other in that way—an important lesson for the growth of an independent lifestyle.

I recently heard a report of some research into brain function in people with autism. At the deepest level, they are identical with us NTs in that they have feelings and perceptions. This can be measured in real time using a scanner. At the secondary level, we recognise that we have feelings, and there is some drop off in the ability of people with autism here, but it is at the third level that they have a tendency to a significantly reduced ability. At this level, structurally the highest and the closest to the surface of the brain, we NTs can think about the feeling we have, whilst the ASD population are much less able to do this. So it may be fairer to use behavioural techniques with people in this group, as they tend to be less aware of their feelings in terms of patterns, and less aware of the effect of their behaviour on others. Negotiations and reason may not be so relevant to those who are without the necessary neural machinery.

So here is the simple procedure that will undoubtedly work:

- Define the precise behaviour you want to reduce or eliminate; call it X.
- Define a different piece of desirable behaviour which is within the subject's capability but not in her or his daily repertoire; call it Y.
- Observe the subject and note when X occurs, with whom, and where. Most importantly, observe what happens next and what happened immediately before. Continue this until a pattern emerges.

The pattern can be described:

Antecedent (what happened before X)
Behaviour (X)
Consequence (what happens next)

Now all you have to do is:

- Manage the antecedent in a different way (for instance, it might be a specific person entering, or going to a specific location, or a particular activity) if this is relevant.
- Ignore X, ensuring that the consequence is only delivered in response to Y.
- Deliver the consequence in a way that encourages Y.
- Persevere until you get what you want.

There are complications, of course. One is that this is essentially teamwork, and the team needs to be onside because inconsistency is the death of this approach. This is hard because it can feel very cruel: there is no discussion, nor any of the usual "naughty boy" routines. One day things just change. This is very foreign to us NTs, especially those who choose the parent-child model as a basis for interaction with the subject.

Ignoring behaviour is sometimes a difficult thing: the lad with whom I learnt this technique used to spit in our eyes when the going got tough, after which he would try pulling other children's hair, then resort to wetting his trousers and producing surprising amounts of phlegm out of his nose, which he mixed with the urine on his trousers, producing a truly unwelcome and unique shiny texture. Then he would start to throw furniture. Hard to ignore. Using a different example, it is organisationally quite difficult to ignore accumulating washing up or midnight threats of violence.

There are some things that are impossible to ignore, and you need a strategy to maintain your emotional and physical health through this time, though things can quickly improve. When you feel you have to step in, it is vital to ensure that the desired consequence still only arrives in response to the new behaviour Y. Also, not to complicate this unconscious learning, it is important to stay safe with the minimum disruption. In school, it is relatively easy to develop a strategy for getting the disruptive and distressed pupil out of the classroom with minimum damage but avoiding the reward. It is much harder in a domestic situation, and equally important to avoid bribery (in effect protection money—if I give you this, will you please desist?). Bribes confuse because they are not immediate, and reward the undesired behaviour in that payments cease if the threat vanishes. They are a conscious strategy, and not an effective one, while consequences (which I will discuss shortly) are also conscious, but more effective. This behavioural strategy is essentially one of retraining unconscious behaviour through precise administration of desired rewards. Better to manage the antecedent and intervene early in order to minimise the disruption: get him out when he spits rather than wait for the flying chairs. Better to intervene over one mug than a week's festering washing up.

The next complication is that inevitably, and rather frighteningly, as the campaign progresses and starts to work, the subject challenges the new boundary, so that undesirable behaviour X increases rather than decreases. Hidden away behind the one-way glass at the end of the classroom, it is easy to enjoy this as a sign of early success. It is true in my experience that it takes about six weeks to get to a better place, and that in those six weeks things get a lot worse before they get better. In my personal subjective experience, it seems that things go just beyond the point where everyone wants to stop, and I suppose the sense of that is that you have to break new ground in order to move forward, and the team feels the pressure no less than the subject.

From the safe place behind the glass, we know that any change in the "baseline incidence" of the behaviour is good as it presages change, and given that the consequence or reward is consistently applied to the desired behaviour Y, success will come. However, if you are dealing with yet another broken window or assaulted classmate, this may not be tolerable. Strangely, my early success in this came with the most difficult young man who had thirty-two undesirable behaviours. I only worked on one, managing the others as well as possible, and was puzzled when the psychologist encouraged me to take the least important behaviour. We did the work, and all thirty-two pieces of behaviour reduced beyond all expectations. Simply, this was because he wanted my attention, and he got it just for sitting next to me with both feet on the floor.

Jason was eight when I met him, and he was the champion spitter and No. 1 difficult child in a school for autistic children. He had no speech and was very autistic. His educational psychologist, who later rescued me, said: "I knew something was up when I first met him and his parents locked my office door as they brought him in." I was new to teaching, and as soon as I took over his class of six boys, he began to get more difficult. He lost interest, started to fiddle with his shoelace, and this rapidly escalated to him pulling other people's hair, crying, "snottering", throwing furniture over and running away from me, so I had to go and get him from the corridors and other classrooms in the school. The educational psychologist was called in, watched the mayhem, and told me that Jason was working for my attention. I found that hard to believe—he kept running away from me. The psychologist asked me to list all Jason's unwanted behaviours. I listed 32 of them, starting with the shoelaces and ending with the running out of the classroom. Following instructions with gritted teeth, I ignored all but the first of these behaviours (shoelace fiddling). I always sat him next to me, and as I taught the group with the help of my good friend and teaching assistant, I turned to him every minute, touched him and said his name.

All other behaviours were ignored and dealt with by my assistant if possible. Things got worse for about six weeks, then improved, and then all 32 behaviours virtually vanished and Jason became comparatively compliant, especially for me.

As I write this I am thinking of work with young children with autism—that was my experience. I know that it is possible to implement this successfully with anyone (try it on your partner!). Apparently, or perhaps apocryphally, a class of psychology students conducted an experiment. The subject was, of course, the lecturer. Behaviour X (to be eradicated) was for him to stand in the left half of the classroom. Desirable behaviour Y was for him to stand in the right half. Lecturers like to think their students are rapt, intrigued and happy (poor well-intentioned saps that they are), and the class response to X was fidgeting, closing books, whispering, etc. Conversely, if he wandered, confused and anxious at his poor delivery, over the line and into the right half of his teaching space into behaviour Y, they were all bright-eyed, rapt and breathlessly hanging on to his every word. He ended up teaching from the right hand wall, no doubt nonchalantly leaning on it. Although they had him exactly where they wanted him, he was doubtless relieved, and strengthened in his belief in his extraordinary teaching prowess. "Had a good day at work dear?"

However, this approach is not a popular way for families to work. Parents usually hate doing it and break the requirements, and the subject, especially if he is an adolescent with Asperger's, argues and complains, and usually wins the point. It is also difficult for families to manage violence or threats thereof.

Tip No 63: Teamwork
Working together feels good

This is not to say that it is not relevant, because it is. This route is the most likely to get the result you want. It is a very effective and speedy way of retraining unconscious behaviour. It may not work for everyone, but this will probably be because the team (or family) finds it too difficult to maintain consistently, and it may be that a verbal person will bring argument into play and try to debate the situation back into her or his favour (often successfully, in my experience). I have some alternative strategies to share in a moment, but first it seems important to note that it is probably better not to start a behavioural campaign unless you are able and willing to carry it out in a highly consistent way, no matter what, for at least two months. This will mean all sorts of fail-safe mechanisms being designed, so that you can manage the short-term consequences of the change in boundaries being implemented whilst staying safe and minimising stress.

So imagine that no one is at fault and everyone is trying their best. It is just that there are conflicting needs, expectations and ambitions. In this scenario, each person is responsible for getting what she or he wants, or at least finding the serenity to accept those things that cannot be changed.

The first strategy required to bring this scenario to life is to become clear about what you do want. It is easy to stay in the moment and make all efforts to accept the unacceptable, to sacrifice your perspective and try to see it from his point of view. The problem is that sometimes this gives space for the other person to develop some increasingly deviant behaviour. Also, eventually most people snap and renege on their previous tolerance, which seems unfair in the short term. In truth, this is the coward's way out, apparently being loving and understanding but actually not being willing to share the wisdom of your point of view, and withholding the truth about your slowly simmering volcano of dissatisfaction. Better to step back and take a long slow look at where it has all come from, what it is like and where it is all going next. This shift in time frames will help you to assess what is acceptable and what is not, as will a step back, which is best achieved by physically going to another space, possibly talking with a friend, possibly taking a walk to give yourself thinking space. Consider what your dream life would be like, and note the differences. Accept the wisdom from God to discriminate between what can and what can't be changed, and the serenity to accept what can't be changed—but be parsimonious in this: most things can be changed, though the consequences of the change may not always be exactly what you envisage.

The necessary courage to change what can be changed starts with assertiveness: saying very clearly what you want. There is a whole school of assertiveness, so all I will offer is a few useful formulations from that school. All of them require that you keep your cool, avoid interpretation and look after yourself.

The Broken Record Technique asks that you endlessly repeat what you want no matter what happens. For example:

"I want you do your share of the washing up from today."
"Yes, OK."
"So I want to do this washing up now, please."
"I'll do it in a minute."
"I hear you, and I want you to do it now, please."
"But it isn't all mine."
"No it isn't, and I want you to do this washing up now, please."
"That isn't fair."
"You don't think that's fair, and I want you do this washing up now, please."
"But I'm in the middle of Doctor Who!"
"I know you're in the middle of Doctor Who, and I want you to do this washing up now, please."

And so on. There is a danger of escalation in this, and you can do your bit to avoid this by avoiding any of the sidetracks, keeping very cool, and sticking solely to your point and nothing else. It works wonderfully in shops where there is less danger of escalation and the customer is always right, but it is perhaps more difficult at home. *Dr Who* (a sci-fi TV programme in the UK) is rather good after all.

Another useful technique is a clear formulation which goes like this:

When you do X, I feel Y, and Z happens. Please do A instead. Will you?

For instance:

"When you leave the towels on the floor I feel disappointed and angry, and I just pick them up and think bad thoughts about you. Please hang them up after you use them. Will you do that?"

"When you stay in bed until 11 o'clock I feel worried and helpless, and then when you do get up I have a go at you and we end up rowing. Please will you start to get up before Dad goes to work so we can all have breakfast together? Will you do that?"

Of course the subject has a range of responses, but actually only three:

He could say "No." Then you know where you are and can consider whether you want to push it further, into a behavioural campaign as described above, or use other strategies described below, probably focused on consequences.

Alternatively, he might agree, in which case you can offer to help him to adopt a new habit or leave him alone to get on with it. Again, you know where you are and can move forward—though of course he may not actually turn this into behaviour, but you can deal with that when and if.

The third possible option is to make a counter offer, leading into the land of negotiation. You then have to consider what is important to you and think about your motivation on a deeper level.

- Seeing Dad before he goes to work? Would it be OK to do this in the evening in some new way?
- Having breakfast together? Is it all three of you, or would it be enough if it were you two?
- Getting up at a "reasonable" time? Clarify what you are saying then, accept it isn't about family breakfast at all, and restate your request ("I want you out of bed by 8 o'clock every weekday").
- Redefining what it is that concerns you: is it that he is not doing anything with his life, or that he is up all night disturbing you, or that you want a family event on a regular basis?

The wider thought in assertiveness is that you can be fully responsible for your own actions, but you can only explain to others the effect of their actions on you, ask for a more harmonious way, and see what happens. God grant me . . . Some friends of mine call this "being at cause" rather than "being at effect". "At cause" you are in charge of what you can do and hence you are at the wheel of your own life bus. "At effect", if you let the wheel slip from your grasp and let other people grab it from you, this leaves you as a rather helpless victim of their hijacking.

A rather less brutal thought arising from this is to ensure you are fully responsible for your own actions and responses. Assertiveness helps you to be responsible for sharing your reactions to the others. Taking time out to consider what you really want helps you to be clear about what you need to express assertively. Part of this is saying "No" and meaning it. "No" is an underused word, it seems to me. People find easier ways to get round a difficult prospect, saying "Yes" instead, for instance, and then grinning and bearing it. There are probably cultural differences here: for instance Americans are reputedly better at saying no, whilst the Brits major in "grin and bear it", but I note that assertiveness arose from American writing, contemporaneously with NLP as it happens.

Apart from changing the subject artfully and going into denial, the other option is to hedge your bets and confuse the issue. Many people seem to dislike sharing clarity about their preferences. The key is to take your time to discover how you really feel about the proposed course of action.

Tip No 64: Problem solving
Identify the problem clearly

Tip No 65: Saying No
Say it you mean it, mean it if you say it

It sometimes comes down to a negotiation of some sort, and the desired result in a negotiation is that every party leaves the discussion feeling at least that the compromises are fairly shared. Some people with Asperger's are strong negotiators. Some are so strong, in fact, that they give nothing away at all, becoming dictators within their families. As a parent, partner, friend or sibling, it is an appropriate response to pull out of a negotiation if there is no chance of compromise being reached. Time for something stronger.

A more cerebral approach is to use the concept of consequences, in which the outcome of a certain piece of behaviour is logical and undesirable. This is subtly different to punishment. The consequence for dropped towels is that that next time he has damp, dirty towels (or no towels) to use. Not doing the washing up could bring the consequence that you stop cooking for him, or that he is not allowed to use the kitchen, or that the TV is controlled so *Dr Who* cannot interrupt the process.

Staying in bed in the morning could bring the consequence that he got a cold flannel dropped on his head at 7.30, or his duvet swiped from him. Not finding time for a family breakfast might result in there being no breakfast available, or your refusal to drive him somewhere, or some withdrawal of your attention when he does drag himself out. The ultimate consequence is the rule of law, of course. "If you hit me again I will call the police."

The key to the consequences approach is that it puts the ball in his court: "If you do this, the consequence is this. It is your choice." There is also a strong link to the notion of connectedness: no matter what you do or choose not to do, consequences flow. There is always a choice, and you make it by your choice of action (or inaction). The consequences that arise become clearer when you vary the time frame of consideration: even if a young man in his twenties or thirties, living at home with his parents, continues to avoid any involvement in planning his future and taking action that will open up wider choices (managing his money, learning to interact with strangers, do house-work etc.), it is still an undeniable fact that he will end up having to change when his parents become too old to continue taking the load off his shoulders.

In all of these strategies and techniques, the subject will feel the urge to challenge the new boundary. We all like predictable patterns, and the behaviours we are trying to reduce or eliminate are usually (though superficially) to the subject's advantage, so he will be reluctant to give them up. This implies that you need to be sure you have the courage to change those things that are open to change. These techniques are designed to make it easier for you to do so, but of course you also like predictable patterns and so are probably reticent about your choices, preferences and feelings, which is why coaching is such a necessary resource.

CHAPTER THIRTEEN

Coaching people forward

Coaching people forward to generate better conditions for themselves requires a specific dynamic, and is probably the subject of a great deal of the coaching literature that already exists. One of the differences between coaching Asperger's and coaching NTs is that people with Asperger's often live closer to crisis: much coaching, although it does of course relate to changing behaviour and moving forward to success, focuses more on the forward movement than the abyss.

Moving forward is partly about goals, and I have already written all I need to about goal setting: that process alone can carry coaching forward. This section is more about making the choices that generate and motivate the strategy.

Actually, most people with Asperger's often have quite reasonable dreams for themselves which may (if you want to be critical) be a little stereotypical, but are by definition well within the range most of us consider as an acceptable future. I want to explore what can be done to make these dreams achievable, and what constitutes a balanced and acceptable way of life. I also want to take into account some of the ways in which people with Asperger's tend to subvert the usual pattern of life, and the possible consequences of these subversions. We are now moving the focus away from the more severe problems, where the need for change is more obvious, and towards the area in which the desired change is generative and creative rather than curative.

People have different motivations. Some will only respond to a crisis: perhaps they become so accustomed to this pressure around a crisis that they become desensitised to the less strident possibilities. Many people with Asperger's find it difficult to discover and maintain a sense of their own power—this may be learnt or inherent, but what motivates a passive person to new action? Telling them is not an effective strategy, and it is easy for passive people to agree with what is said without ever letting it stir them into action. The responsibility of the coach is to find a way to motivate the subject, and the coach will be most effective when she or he discovers the thinking style that underpins motivation rather than making an assumption ("it's common sense . . ."). People with Asperger's tend to live in a personal world where they only do what makes sense to them and find it difficult to get behind doing things a different way. They are also traditionally seen as being weak on strategy development. One of the keys to coaching for change, then, is that whatever new action they seek to adopt has to make sense to them. Of course it makes sense to us NTs that getting up early and doing some housework, exercise and shopping are the underpinning bulwarks of a life which will be attractive to others, but . . . "I'll start tomorrow, what's the difference?"

If he could think his way out of this and into the next phase of life, he would surely have done it by now, wouldn't he? If you are dissatisfied with your situation, you need to do something new and different in order to get something new and different. Selling this to an Aspie depends on the coach finding ways to enable the subject to recognise these truths in his own context.

Most people with Asperger's I have met speak of wanting a wife, a job, a car and a house. Several have most of these; most of them seem not to have the wife (though the ones who have probably do not think to seek me out). However, I have spoken to a few who have achieved all of these acquisitions, though again the natural selection in my sample means I am unlikely to meet many of the satisfied ones. Satisfaction does not necessarily arrive with the acquisition of certain stereotypical ambitions and accoutrements, though.

It takes away the freedom to blame external causes, and may encourage a more reflective consideration of the purpose or meaning an individual attaches to his life if he discovers that external things do not bring happiness.

A dream life: we cynical old NTs know that this is a dream and that real life is full of compromises, negotiations and acceptance of frustration. A normal life might be a better way of labelling this dream, though we also know that a normal life, whilst acknowledging the rights of the individual to make choices, is also constricted by responsibilities. I have had a considerable amount of contact with young men who have Asperger's, and I see that sometimes they are notably unwilling to take on the responsibility side of this equation. Often, to be fair, this is because they feel unable to do so: fear, compulsion and isolation combine to give rise to such strong feelings that all these NT-friendly grey areas become "no go areas" for some Aspies.

We parents know that our children will be happy when they are independent (or is it that we just want that spare room back?). In truth, it is rarely a problem in the NT world because just as parents seem to be programmed to behave like parents, so children are programmed to fight their way free of the suffocation of parental control. Home is that place you can always go back to, and where you want to get away from as fast as you can.

Asperger's syndrome sometimes seems to sabotage this natural desire, and then the family enters into this unknown territory for which none of the inhabitants is prepared. Some may not be able to take on this level of independence, and some families may be happy to continue to live as one interdependent unit. Some will be eager to take the first steps, others reluctant, and those who do make the move will do so as a result of interlocking circumstances which enable this seminal move: work creates income, or a college place creates the need to move out, a certain level of independent choice makes it desirable, perhaps some friends encourage a flat share. Eventually the circumstances alter enough for the scales to tip, and the person moves out. With some people I know, the move has only been created through the intervention or support of the mental health system. On exit from hospital, the authorities set people up in independent circumstances. In the intervening time, parents have come to accept that change is inevitable, as has the child, and everyone has become used to living separately.

All parents keep an eye on their fledglings for a while, sending packages of cake and fruit, offering to continue to do the washing, visiting and accepting the home-cooked pasta, buying towels and pillowcases as surprise presents, and maintaining a view of the standards. This is a stage we all grow out of when we become convinced that the progeny is doing OK (some peculiar eating habits, have you seen . . ., do you think . . ., is he *sleeping* enough?). Girls apparently find a mummy's boy to be a turn-off, probably thinking they are next in line for washing duties, and want their man to be strong and brave and prepared to clean the toilet at least sometimes. So after the big moment when he moves out, parents usually continue to monitor standards until they are convinced. Many people with Asperger's are built to resist this entire process, being highly independent and private people. They do not welcome change, often find it hard to see the sense in doing something that is not immediately necessary, and are not the most open to advice.

However, we all have the right to live a creative life that suits us. Mum says: "Yes, so long as he is eating well and happy"; and Dad says: "Yes, so long as he is getting out, meeting people and getting on with his life." Parents have a wider perspective: their job in life is to share this without imposing it. In terms of coaching forward towards a healthy, satisfying, balanced and sustainable life (I am a parent, so I can allow myself all these adjectives!), there is a negotiation which must lead towards the subject picking up all the reins himself, but he has to earn the right to that freedom by demonstrating his ability to succeed. The major difficulty here is deciding exactly what the parameters of success are for an individual. Assuming he is not damaging himself or others (and this probably includes freeloading on parents), then the most useful measure is his subjective assessment of his satisfaction. A low level of satisfaction indicates potential stress or disappointment; a high level indicates pleasure and pride.

Measuring a balanced life is essentially a subjective process: there is a structure called a "coaching wheel" which allows you to chart your level of satisfaction with all things in your life, represented by the segments of the wheel. If you have a balanced life and are fully satisfied with all areas in it, you have a smooth ride. High scores all round give you a comfortably balanced and evenly shaped wheel for the great journey of life. If some area is less satisfying to you than others, the lower score creates a gap in your wheel, and you get a bumpy ride. However, over the years the number of topics (and the names they go by) has varied a little. There are some obvious ones (health, money) and some more arcane things like spirit, happiness, community. Even allowing for the variability of choice in this area, whichever topics are relevant to you can be put into your model. The idea is that we will do well to achieve a high and equal level of satisfaction in our lives.

This is the version I use:

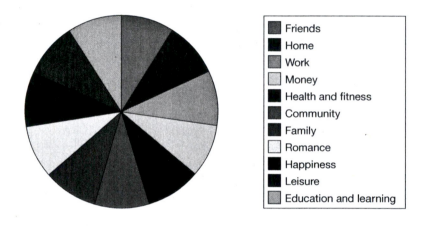

To use the wheel, you mark each section with a satisfaction rating of 1–10. At the centre of the wheel is a small unsatisfactory life, so 1 just scores at the hub. 10 takes you right out to the rim. Whatever your subjective scores are defines whether or not you are having a bumpy ride through life.

However, there is no proper consensus on which topics should be included. There is certainly a cultural model, and probably an individual subjective one too, though there are some topics which cannot be excluded: health and fitness, for instance, and probably something about being connected to people. Asperger's syndrome gives people difficulties in the area of people, but almost all of the Aspies I meet admit that they would like to be more connected in one way or another. I have met a few who would evidently feel better if all the people would just go away, though that in itself may be the result of years of rejection. Alternatively, it may be that the messy

NT world is in fact a construct of our overly connected consciousness, and that some Aspies may well enjoy the solitary life. However, when in Rome . . . There is no definitive answer, and the real measure is what does a person feel comfortable with, what does he hanker for and what does he not enjoy? In some cases people may well be deluding themselves: it might prove to be a horrible experience to have a live-in lover, for instance, moving all your stuff around and wanting you to talk when you don't want to. As with all creative movement, you cannot be sure that where you get to will be what you want until you get there. Balance, however, is good, is it not?

Tip No 66: Specific coaching
Teaching tips

Early on in this process, one has to consider the impact of a decision on those around. Sometimes Aspies seem to find this difficult, and the Triad of Impairments does indicate a difficulty with empathy as a causative feature of this syndrome. Sometimes it is good to reduce the emotional content of this and increase the consequential considerations. Instead of: "Your mum and dad are really tired by this, and worrying so much it is damaging their health", it is some-times more useful to go along lines such as: "You use your parents' money to go out and get drunk, then come back out of control and shout at them. True? If you carry on, they will stop giving you money to go out. If they let it go on, they will get more and more frightened, and will eventually have to call the police to stop you. You'll end up in the cells, in court, and possibly in a psychiatric hospital or prison. Do you want that to happen? So what do you have to do?"

Many people with Asperger's seem to find life quite uncomfort-able. I would love to listen to a group of people with the condition designing their perfect life, and I wonder how different it would be to the NT world in which we live. Maybe this "Anthropologist on Mars" effect is truly disturbing to live with and people would be more comfortable if they could have a life designed around their own styles, but maybe they would be disconnected and lonely. It is a matter for experiment, and we have to acknowledge that the answers may be unexpected. In any case, it is clear that for each individual, some results are more comfortable and satisfying than others, and conversely, it is clear that some responsibilities have to be met whether or not they are comfortable and satisfying. We probably feel better if we have more control over our lives.

If satisfaction, or happiness, is the ambition, then we have to recognise that the achievement of this enlightened state is one of continued exploration: "I'll be happy when I have (wife, car, job, flat tummy . . .). Hmmm. Still not happy! I'll be happy when I have more free time. Hmmm. I'll be happy when I can play the guitar like Clapton. Hmmm. I'll be happy when I can sit down and do nothing but enjoy the sunshine. Hmmm. When the rain stops . . ." We are apparently capable of going round this expedition for several lifetimes. How will you know when you are happy? The answer to this question is entirely individual. Some will say: "When I know I have tried as hard as I can." Others might try: "I won't be happy till the day I die—dissatisfaction keeps me going." Or: "When I want for nothing." Or: "When I have a loving relationship." As a coach, one has to discover the answer to this question and feed the motivation that is identified. All of the coaching tips throughout this book can be applied to the coach as much as the coached, so if the desired motivation does not arise, then a new line of attack is required: if something does not work, try something else.

So this wheel can be useful, as can Mum and Dad's advice and one's own consideration of "I really ought to do this", which leads us back to New Year Resolutions territory. It may be that goals come popping out easily in this consideration, or it may be that the person finds it difficult to generate choices she or he can really sign up to. The thoughts to carry in this process are:

- . If you carry on doing the same things, you will carry on getting the same result.
- If you don't like something in your life, either change it or decide to put up with it.
- You learn by doing: take action to find out what is possible.

Satisfaction is subjective, but it tells you something about your level of expectation and about your sense of values. If you are dissatisfied, you can either stop kvetching and learn to live with it or you can decide to change it. There is no sense in living in the middle bit where you complain but do nothing to change that of which you complain.

However, it is helpful to consider what changes can help you move towards a balanced life.

Tip No 67: Opening doors
Problem planning: what if?

People work in a systemic way: internally, for instance, we have a need for a balanced diet and sufficient exercise. Some people with Asperger's would be well advised to try out a healthy diet, as they may well be sensitive to many additives in our food, and that sensitivity may affect their attention or their level of relaxation. Additionally, they may have adverse reactions to external environmental features or to internal experiences, such as anxiety, which throw their system more off-balance than with much of the NT population. The idea of a system is that you can make a change in one input and affect the entire system: ensuring that the body has the right balance of minerals, for instance, can improve health and energy.

Regular sleep patterns are notoriously easy to lose if you are an Aspie, though not always. Lack of sleep is a major cause of stress and confusion, not only affecting your ability to learn, think and respond, but also damaging your body, so it is an obvious component of a healthy and happy lifestyle. The only answer I know for regular sleep is to adopt regular habits. Absence of caffeine and absence of late night stimulating computer games may make a difference, and a night time routine of reading, listening to the radio or suitably quiet music may help too. However, in the end the thing that makes the biggest difference is whether you are ready for sleep, and this is mostly determined by how many hours you have been awake. So the most effective way to develop a regular sleep pattern is to get up at a regular time, in the reasonably early morning (before 9.00 a.m. in any case). There are also social reasons for adopting this pattern, in that this is the rhythm everyone else follows, and it ensures that you will have had enough of being awake by midnight. Whilst you can control whether you stay awake, you cannot control when you fall asleep, so it is more possible to get yourself out of bed at a set time and deal with any consequent tiredness than it is to go to bed before midnight and fall asleep no matter what. You are best served if you realise that you are training your body to get used to the new rhythm, and that repetition and consistency work best.

Of course you may have to put the clock on the far side of the bedroom!

All other areas in the coaching wheel are offered as possibilities that may affect your systemic self. Managing your money to your own satisfaction, so that you can pay all your bills and still pay for what you want to buy, matters a great deal to most people, and debt is a cause of grinding stress. Of course in every case the balance you achieve is a personal and subjective judgement—do I feel good about my finances? In some cases there may be a gap between the expectations of others and the subject's individual preferences, and it is the responsibility of those around the subject to bring him to a point where he accepts a full level of adult responsibility. Actually the question is more: "Do I feel good about the way I manage my responsibilities?"

Sometimes this process of bringing the person up to accept his responsibilities is not completed and he may slip into a pattern— Asperger's often encourages this by allowing an obsessive compo- nent to develop in the personality. The subject may well claim to enjoy using all his leisure time on computer games, but may actually be better served by spending some of it in the open air, getting used to people and exercising a little. If those around a person can see a better way, they have some level of responsibility to share this information, whether they are parents, friends or work colleagues. However, the person with Asperger's also has a responsibility for the consequences of his or her choices. The basic coaching rule is: "If you don't like what is happening, change what you do until you get a preferable result."

So if you want friendship, you need to find things to share with other people and to let them into your life. There are groups, both in the flesh and online, that cover the widest range of interests. Of course then you have to learn social skills or find people who like you as you are, but you cannot do this until you are with other people.

At this point I am feeling a keen urge to define happiness, or at least progress towards defining it. I am often working to help people move away from what causes unhappiness, and these crises can allow individuals to avoid the more subtle questions (What is happiness? What do I really want in my life?).

Tip No 68: Metaphors
It's like a . . . and I can tell you why!

The positive psychologists may have done the job for me. They suggest that happiness is subjective and is therefore only really open to self-assessment tests, although there are patterns that demonstrate emotional stress so it may be possible to assess happiness observationally (habits, health, education, goals attainment, relationships . . .). They suggest that a time frame of past, present and future may be helpful in this assessment, and that in the present there is a difference between the hedonists who value positive sensual experiences and those who value more enduring gratifications.

Then there is the distinction between the pain avoidance-pleasure seeking principle, which allows behaviourism to be effective, and the alternative one of seeking a way to maximise your potential. This is interesting, and it is helpful because it offers a scientific route for us to move towards understanding and objectifying the study of an essentially subjective experience. There is, of course, much more work being done on examining how to create positive states and attitudes to your own life, and differentiating the various areas of life (as per the coaching wheel above) that influence the overall perception of experience.

As a practitioner, though, I take all this as useful underpinning of my practice. If the individual I work with tells me that he is dissatisfied, I take this at face value. My question arising is always: "So what do you want?" and my route is defined by that answer, as I assume that there is a controlling subconscious intelligence in the individual which is producing a relevant answer. I often use the Well Formed Outcome structure initially to explore exactly what the evidence will be that the subject has reached his goal. The initial result may be that he reaches his objective only to find it is full of features which bring unforeseen dissatisfactions. This is an opportunity to learn, to raise your sights a bit and explore your personal definition of happiness further. So you want a nice flash car, you work hard, get it, and find that you still feel incomplete. You need a person in the passenger seat perhaps, or maybe you lost your focus on the balanced life and spent all your time getting the car, missing the need you have to be fit and healthy. So long as I successfully make the point that coaching is an exploration for each individual (coach and subject) of what is possible and desirable for the subject, and that the subject is responsible for the consequences of his actions and is capable of more than he has previously achieved, I am content. Or happy, perhaps. Whole philosophies and religions are built on the bigger questions, and although it seems to me that they largely overlap, wars are fought over who is right and who is not. All I know is that a sense of direction from "don't like" to "do like" is a good way to explore your own personal sense of meaning.

Tip No 69: Being artfully vague: Milton model

When you notice how you are relaxing right now . . . when you feel good with me in our safe space . . . when you feel like that . . .

So coaching someone towards a goal involves enabling him to define a wholesome goal which fits his perception of the world he inhabits. Without this there will be no motivation. This may include altering time frames, including consideration of other people's wants, hopes and aspirations, and it may also include some exercise of assertiveness to renegotiate expectations. There may also need to be consideration of how to manage the reactive and pressing needs of a crisis (usually short-term) towards building a long-term proactive plan to move towards a chosen goal. However, it is not helpful to overlook the short-term pressing needs, so it is necessary to balance time demands and multitasking. The coaching wheel is a way to explore these competing demands.

Asperger's syndrome brings its own dynamic to these manoeuvrings because it appears to enhance the ability we all have to ignore the middle term space in which we develop and operate strategies of new behaviour that move from the familiar to the new. The condition may also allow the development of highly idiosyncratic thinking patterns in which common sense is defeated by cold logic, and it is more likely to be a successful strategy to match the coaching process to the idiosyncratic style rather than to change the person's mind. Failure to reach the desired end is a learning point, of course, and it is absolutely necessary to support the person through this so that failure is not perceived as proof of inadequacy but used as a spur for further learning.

CHAPTER FOURTEEN

Coaching out of crisis

L eft unsupported, people with Asperger's often drift into negativity and harmful thinking patterns, sometimes leading to breakdown or collapse of confidence. I have had a lot of experience in attempting to coach people forward from this position, which is a rather specialised process. This specialisation is one of the most stressful areas of work for me, although it is largely and prosaically no more than very intensive listening and reflecting. Often a strong crisis is associated with a level of obsessive-compulsive thinking, paranoia and other distorted thinking. The particular level of listening required is a highly adapted one of acceptance with boundaries. For a relationship to be healthy, both parties have to be themselves and not feel constrained or pushed into the other person's map of the world. I have sometimes found myself tied in emotional knots when a client of mine can only accept the other person agreeing with his or her point of view. It is rare and extreme to find someone who completely insists on total agreement, but it is well within my experience in this population. Fortunately, most people I meet have not gone so far down the road, although many cannot tolerate direct disagreement without wanting to run or fight.

I am useless to them if I pretend to agree, and they make me useless to them if I disagree and experience a high level of stress in discovering the correct route though this particular needle eye. Rapport is an essential state to reach before it is possible to move forward, though, and a route has to be found. "I understand that you feel . . ." is a route, but a highly obvious one, and I am usually ambushed if I try it. "You are really, really, REALLY upset by this . . ." is much better, as it stresses the other person's emotion. Non-verbal messages which stress acceptance are useful (uncrossed arms, nodding, repeated use of exact vocabulary), but in truth this is a difficult position, and the more exact I try to be, the greater the stress—but also the greater the payoff in terms of trust development.

People in crisis are experiencing inner turmoil: their thoughts are incoherent, their feelings are strong, their feeling of control weak. I have visited people newly arrived—against their will—in psychiatric wards, prison cells and the back rooms of family friends, and the first thing required in order to open up the possibility of more generative coaching is an overdose of listening with minimum steerage: corrections, reality checks and disagreement can all bring the conversation to a close, and where is it the value in that?

These are extreme moments. More often I find myself seeing the crisis coming and trying to help people avoid the most damaging experiences in favour of compromise and negotiation. Sometimes, in contrast, I find myself waiting for the crisis which will in fact break the Gordian knot and create new circumstances which will enable people to move forward. Let the chips fall where they will.

Some crises are immediate, others more of a slow burn. The depressed and isolated person living in his bedroom, unwilling to come out and mix, is steering himself slowly to a crisis through his inaction. He has to come to see this for himself, and sometimes it is only the crisis that makes the point.

Two essential presuppositions of coaching are:

The person is doing the best he can at the moment.
When he sees a better way, he will take it.

For change to happen, he needs to help in clarifying his goals and ambitions. This is difficult even to contemplate when you are depressed, paranoid, angry and anxious. I find that a large amount of my coaching energy has, over the years, gone to waiting for a change in these emotional circumstances. Maybe this does not have to be so, and maybe there are techniques (such as brief therapy, reframing, challenge and sleight of mouth) which will create rapid change, but I tend to believe that strong beliefs give rise to powerful reference experiences which require equally strong experiences to create the tipping point where belief change happens. The way a strong crisis fades into the background is by the slow "drip, drip, drip" of small-scale positive experiences over a long time. Eventually, people will begin to see that there is a different way. Coaching can speed this process, and it may be that the crisis point is not the optimum time to begin coaching. Crises happen, however, and circumstances change rapidly at this point. Coaching can, if nothing else, encourage acceptance and use of the new perspectives that arise as old doors close and new ones open. We coaches are so positive that sometimes we are the only ones who can see the possibilities arising from a sudden crisis.

There is a healing process for each person to discover personally, and this can be supported by the presence of a coach whose job at all times is to help the subject to grapple with reality so he can develop a route to a more desirable place. Facts and emotions are different, of course, though we all tend to believe our emotional judgements. Emotions are true, but different people in the same circumstances can have opposite emotions at identical moments. As we say: "The map is not the territory." What you think and feel about an experience is not the experience itself. Under stress we have an increased hold on the familiar—we are creatures who value consistency and pattern, after all. Often all those around the crisis have a resistance to it: it can feel like sitting on top of a hill watching a thunderstorm coming, knowing that you are about to get very wet, not wanting to, but having nowhere to run, nowhere to hide. Coaching the system can sometimes include encouraging a person to call time on an unacceptable piece of behaviour. Let the chips fall where they will—very little is worth avoiding at all costs.

Specific features which sometimes come along with Asperger's and which are helpful to move away from include depression, paranoia, anger, anxiety, fear. They are all systemic recipes mixing emotion, thought and belief, which direct and control behaviour in an unhelpful way. To work with them positively, I use rapport as a starting place, which may in fact be all that is needed, and over a considerable amount of time it may allow the person to find a self-healing route. I support this by focusing on acceptance, ownership of the circumstance, and possibilities, so that choices can be identified and power returned to the owner of the life.

The linguistic tools around distortion, generalisation and deletion are probably the main tools I use, inviting the person to explore the falsity of the connections he perceives. However, rejection of the person's position is unhelpful; hence my persistence with rapport as the main tool. Not only are the feelings and thought patterns deeply held and highly self-supporting, they may be inherent. In my experience it is often powerful to admit that this pattern isn't going away, and it can be more helpful to coach a person to accept the experience than to attempt to move him out of it.

Medication has to be mentioned as a helpful strategy. Aspies are rather prone to contra-indication in which the usual medication produces an unusual response, and there are both side effects and the dangers of addiction to be wrestled with. I am no friend of chemical intervention, as I fear it is less well understood than we are told, and persistence of prescription sometimes arises for non-patient-friendly reasons. However, new medicines are constantly being developed, and many of them have a strongly beneficial effect which can create a doorway into a more positive experience. When you controls anxiety, the world becomes a different place, and every day is brighter. Maybe it is then possible to learn new behaviours and use the resulting increase in positive feelings to support an eventual withdrawal of the medication. I have seen this happen, and it seems to be an entirely valid treatment strategy.

Resulting from these negative feelings (or perhaps quite separately from them), behavioural patterns can arise from which the person needs to escape. These will include isolation, dependency and perhaps breakdown, in which he changes his behaviour dramatically and becomes suddenly much less able to manage his life, and which brings him into the category of crisis.

Conditions of life and lifestyle choices such as isolation and dependency need to be addressed, and the techniques I have written about are all useful. Crucially, those around the person must become active and avoid collusion, heightening his awareness of the discomfort inherent in the choices he is making. The intention is to ensure that motivation is created by an awareness of the consequences of the choices and how the responsibility for these consequences rests with the subject.

PART III

SPECIFIC ISSUES

INTRODUCTION

This third part of the book gives me space to look briefly at some specific issues. In truth they are each worthy of a book in their own right, but it would be a serious omission to leave them entirely for later: these are the issues with which people with Asperger's are most concerned. Each offers a personal view, and some will not be relevant to some people, of course, but in my experience these are all "hot" issues, and parents may well also benefit from taking a long cool look at them.

I am aware that all these issues could be solved by a mega-dose of self-esteem, but I am also aware that self-esteem is something of a magic elixir, the possession of which sorts out all problems. We NTs have problems in these areas as well, and we know that a big dose of self-esteem would help us out too. The difference is still profound, however: whilst we NTs may have problems in (some of) these issues, we generally manage, and we know what we are doing wrong if we fail for a while. Aspies often seem to be entirely left out, without a conception of what they are doing wrong or what they could do right. Theirs is a qualitative problem in which they have little notion of what they lack. Ours are quantitative in that we know perhaps that we are a bit down on social skills (this week). So it is not just self-esteem they need, but much more an injection of specific experiences that will help them to develop positive thoughts and feelings.

144

CHAPTER FIFTEEN

Social skills

W hat is the Christmas party for? Well, as Tony said: "I am often amazed at how NTs waste their time looking after each other, stroking each other." The group experience gives us NTs a chance to make sure that others are feeling good, to check out how they feel about us, to enjoy that ephemeral connection which seems to live in a wine bottle, and to gain a bit of advantage by being noticed.

Specifically, we give a lot of eye contact: some of it asked for, some of it not asked for, some of it withheld. We rub a lot of shoulders, laugh at a lot of bad jokes, and create a mini-myth for the four or five hours we are in the arena. Until about 10.30 we also listen to each other; after that we approximate our verbal inputs to the last person's, or just make people laugh. Or just laugh. In this myth we like each other, enjoy each other's humour, get interested in the things they do and the people they know. We do a major rapport dance in which we somehow enhance each other's good feelings, in which we are somehow included. We let our hair down a little in order to share some feeling of intimacy, and then we usually go home to our partners—but sometimes we "go for a coffee".

The thing is, we do all of this unconsciously, and can rapidly see through those who for one reason or another are acting. We hate nothing more than the hypocrisy of people being insincere. The social skills we all use are unconscious and hard to teach—hard to adopt if you don't talk the language. They are essentially responsive and interactive. Too much staring is uncomfortable (how would you know?). Too much eye avoidance is shifty, private, threatening (how do you know what people think of you when you are not even looking?).

Tip No 70: Creating "feelgood"
Lean on me

Research suggests that many people with Asperger's tend to watch only the mouth in a conversation, avoiding all reference to the eyes, face, shoulders, and so on. When you attempt a conversation in which you only watch the other person's mouth, you realise how disadvantaging it is. When listening, you have no clues as to when to speak except when the mouth shuts up. Small pause (while you wonder what to say) in which someone else pipes up and interrupts your thought-out, intelligent (and slightly late) response. When you are talking, of course, you never get the signal to stop and let the other person chip in, because that does not come from the mouth, more from the eyes, hands, shoulders and body position, so you go on until the other person is bored and ready to interrupt you. This, though debilitating in itself, only concerns conversational reciprocity. There is much more to study about the content of what you say, how you say it, the hidden meaning, what you leave unsaid, and so on. This is multi-channel communication, and Aspies are notable for being single trackers, one piece of information at a time. There are theories about why communication is difficult for people with Asperger's, but they remain theories. It may be learned from early failure in those highly competitive teenage years, or it might be neurological in some way.

However, social skills go much deeper, including politeness, body placement, gesture, and empathy. Again, Aspies seem to have real and deep difficulties in knowing what the other person feels. How would you know? Well, the "shadow neurons" tend to produce the feeling that you observe in the other person, and it may be that in Asperger's these neurons don't work too well. Or it may be a translation thing: it is hard to understand what you do not experience. The three levels of emotional experience that arise from brain architecture and function don't work so well in Aspies, so they have feelings like NTs, awareness of those feelings if they are lucky, but very little chance of being able to reflect on these feelings. How would you know what someone else is feeling if you don't have that information within yourself about your own experience?

So teaching social skills is not easy, although there may well be coping skills you can share which alleviate the intrinsic difficulty. Other people give good clues, of course, so it may be possible to estimate how far others stand away from someone, for instance, in order to estimate your own particular correct distance. You could learn to nod quite easily, and would then be known as someone who was a good listener. Social procedural rules, such as "take coat, offer tea, indicate seat, make tea, talk about journey", can be really helpful. Sometimes a prompt sheet written down on the kitchen work surface helps. Simple unspoken demonstration does not—it is much more effective and helpful to state overtly "do what I do" than to hope that the habit is in some way catching.

All this is superficial, however: the real way to learn social skills is to find your way into a social situation in which you are comfortable and can make mistakes without cringing. However, it must be said that a group of NTs offers a better learning environment than a group of Aspies. Similarly, it will be easier to learn conversational French from a group of friendly French people than from a group of English speakers, because the former can already speak French. Of course, they also need to be sympathetic and able to deconstruct their language for the benefit of the student, who will still need to be quick on the uptake and big on self-confidence.

Annie says: "The difference between autism and Asperger's is that autistic people are behind a brick wall: they can't see what goes on the other side. Asperger's is like being behind a translucent wall with a few bricks taken out: you can sort of see, and in some areas you can see perfectly well. To help, NTs need to stick their arms right through those holes."

Social skills only really work if they are applied unconsciously. Conscious application does not work too well. Practice is the only real answer, and that practice needs to be done in sympathetic circumstances so that any mistakes and failures can easily be turned into learning experiences. I have taken part in a few improvisational acting classes in my time, and these might be useful. The techniques are all good and easy, and lead you to create new outcomes with very little pain, once you have accepted that you are acting. The framework of a class makes this very easy, of course, and the concepts are useful: everything the other person says is an offer which you can accept in order to keep the flow going—NTs love flow. Status is powerful and very easy to express non-verbally (John Cleese does high status very well, whilst Michael Palin readily goes down to low status), and can be used to get yourself out of trouble with a laugh—NTs love a laugh. The thing about status is that it is in the eye of the beholder. Hold yourself up straight, don't wriggle about, speak slowly and clearly, and people will tend to defer. Alternatively, wriggle about, be shifty, apologise unreservedly (think Baldrick), and you become too demeaning to kick and are excused, contemptuously, but excused nonetheless. It's all in the body language, and that physicality does in fact affect how you feel.

So some skills can be taught, but the practice needs to be among sympathetic people who themselves know what is going on. If in doubt, tell the person exactly what to do—this is what happens when you are presented to the Queen, I am told.

Tip No 71: Building recall
What did you see, hear, feel, smell, taste . . . ?

CHAPTER SIXTEEN

Addiction and habit

Some people are prone to addiction and threaten their own health and welfare with their habits, which become very unbalanced. Sometimes the ensuing damage sucks in family members. Others just enjoy their habits, but sometimes the habits become unhealthy in a more controlled, obsessive-compulsive way. These patterns are not exclusive to the population of people with Asperger's—far from it in fact: there are NT alcoholics and drug takers and people who exercise so much that they damage their hearts, legs and spines. Sometimes the habits are illegal (or the substances are: marijuana, ecstasy and the rest). More often they are legal, though the results can be less so (drunken violence, shoplifting). Sometimes they are undesirable and often they are expensive—pornography can take a lot of money out of your pocket very quickly and damage your fantasy world of relationships. There may also be a social component of the risk (drug dealers can turn into fantasy friends who are really connected to you, but only on condition that you make your regular purchase).

People with Asperger's can be prone to these risks. Some of them are non-compliant with rules and regulations unless they see the point, not worrying too much about the rule-breaking aspect of addiction. Many Aspies are seriously vulnerable to patterns and habits, and can build routines from which they cannot then escape. I have known of people (especially youngsters, perhaps) who develop an exercise habit which seems to outside observers to verge on threatening their health.

I should also mention computers, of course. I am not of an age to be familiar with the games or with the lifestyle where you have a serious social commitment to your keyboard and screen, but I do understand that many younger people have a different model of the world which features the computer much more heavily than my old fashioned version. As with the other varieties of addiction, I can see that this provides an attractive alternative way of life to an Aspie who is socially uncomfortable and unsuccessful in hanging out with people. Many people with Asperger's have empty space in their lives, I suppose (which NTs fill up with meeting people, going out, being in crowds), and it makes complete sense to me that a drink or a puff or a long gaming session might fill the space quite effectively.

I am not going to explore the nature of addiction; I will just consider briefly what can be done to help individuals to continue to seek a healthy, balanced life when they are seemingly caught up in an unbalanced and unhealthy pattern of behaviour. There is only one serious question, and it is a very difficult one to answer: does it matter? Family expectations are powerful, and how many times have we heard of a young man breaking his family rules? Even Prince Charles was blamed when he was caught with an underage cherry brandy in his youth. Some families allow a little drug taking, or at least turn a blind eye to it. Most allow drinking. The majority of men have looked at pornography. Many of us have stayed up late doing whatever it is we do: writing this book, for instance, has kept me up late, but then so have guitar playing, friends and parties in my time.

One simple answer to the question (does it matter?) is to look at the financial cost involved, and if the finances fail to add up, then it does. Many youngsters with Asperger's seem to build a financial dependence on their parents which goes on rather longer than the NT model. The simple fact of financial consequences only works if the person is using his money to buy food, pay the rent, bills and all the rest of a regular domestic budget. There is often rather more disposable cash than there should be to encourage true financial responsibility, and if it is spare, then spending it on pornography, alcohol or a spliff is more difficult to argue against. "I don't like this is in my home" is a very real argument, but not a strong enough one. The way to learn the value of money is to learn to ration it and pay your way in the world.

Continuing to look at the habits from the outside, it may be possible for those around the person to see that the habit is isolating him (computer games), leading to his moral corruption (pornography), messing with his health and sleep patterns (drugs and alcohol), or threatening his continuing health (over-exercise). It may also appear that a dependency is building up which the person is unable to see.

Looked at from the first person, it may be possible to see that any of the above is happening, but it is more difficult to get this perspective. Habits and addictions tend to create a blindness which stops the person from seeing the facts clearly. To monitor yourself is difficult, but not impossible. A diary or journal is a good tool to use as it reveals patterns: How often do I buy my grass? Oh, every week now! Whoops! How much did I spend in the pub last night? Hard to recall, but if you empty your pockets of change and put £40 in your wallet before you go, all you have to do is to count the change in the morning. Motivation, however, is crucial: some addictions, especially the chemical ones such as alcohol and drugs, but also pornography, tend to become self-perpetuating by developing a need. Feed the habit. It is then hard to unearth the motivation even to keep a record of your behaviour. Outside help (coaching) is really helpful if this is so.

Classically, addicts tend to wake up every now and then, recognise how far they are falling, and make an effort, creating considerable stress as they try to walk away from this relationship with the bottle, the spliff, the needle. They are not too good at handling stress, though, which is why they fell into the habit in the first place, so it rapidly becomes intolerable to them. Another one bites the dust. The New Year Resolution syndrome writ large. How many times do you have to try before you either give up trying or make the effort actually to cross the great divide?

There is an answer to this classical pattern, which is that those around have to let the person go until he finally makes the momentous choice and starts to seek help and engage with it in a way that leads him out of the need for chemical support. Tough Love is a policy that focuses long and hard on the reality of the consequences of an individual's actions. Co-dependence looms large in this scenario, as family members tend to rally round, trying to show how they care in order to save the person from falling so far that he is unable to climb back, committing the rest of his (now short) life to short-term oblivion until it becomes long-term. With Tough Love, though, it is essential to recognise that support is crucial. Alcoholics Anonymous is an example of a serious commitment to support the individual: non-judgemental, connected, committed, and experienced. There are other services, philosophies and groups, of course, and no single solution seems to have the patent on effective support. Support may be crucial for the families and other co-dependents of course, who face many of the same issues in themselves. No one can deal with an issue for you; you have to do it yourself.

There is a strong thought behind this, and I am not sure if it is the most nihilistic thought imaginable ("no one can do it for you, so you are stuffed unless you can find it in yourself to rescue yourself") or a wonderfully humanitarian thing ("everyone has the strength to rescue themselves, and with the love and support of others they will find it"). I raise this because I am not sure that people with Asperger's have easy access to the Rescuer Within—I am reminded again of that graphic description: "When I look inside myself all I see is a big black hole."

What I do experience is that many Aspies I meet have a difficulty accessing the deeper side of their personality. When I work with NTs and make NLP enquiries, I get more coherent and revealing answers more easily, and one of the presuppositions behind NLP is that "the unconscious mind is benevolent". This is evidenced by the fact that the unconscious mind is part of the being and so will not threaten its own existence. More down to earthly, it clearly acts in extremis to get us out of bad situations (panic, knee-jerk reactions), and it maintains a reasonable level of bodily function (tells us when to sleep, when to eat, what to eat, etc). Many of these functions are affected in many Aspies, though, and it may be that the channels of communication from the basic level to the higher levels of consciousness are tangled in Asperger's syndrome. If so, they may be more vulnerable to addiction and destructive habits and less equipped to find their way out. This cannot be said with any level of certainty— it may also be that they are responding to their experiences in building up ways of avoiding psychological pain which then take up residence.

So it may be that a greater level of intervention is required. I am sure the best we can do here is to assume that every individual is unique and is held in a unique family structure which will work out the best that it can uniquely do. If intervention is decided upon, then it should be effective, and this will be more likely if it is early, seeking to make a difference before the habits become ingrained.

All of the suggestions in the coaching section of this book are available, and the caution I offer is that it will be more effective to choose an intervention that makes sense to the subject. It is a matter of choice whether this is the sense of consequences ("I choose that if you do this, we will do that") or of experience ("If you spend it all on booze then you won't have enough to pay your mobile phone bill") or of competing needs in a balanced life ("If you drink that much, then of course you will feel bad when I wake you up at 8 o'clock—now get up"). What is less likely to work is sweet reason ("I want to talk to you about why pornography is bad for you"). No adverts against drugs ever seem to admit how heroin feels at the time, and it would be a powerful sex education programme that really explored how short-sighted you can become in those intense and private moments.

I come back to the original question: does it matter? Many people live quite well while drinking well over the ever-shrinking suggested limits. Of course it affects their health, and I am not recommending ignoring that, but I do recognise that the individual has personal freedom of choice of diet, exercise and intake regime, and that it seems these choices are taken in a much looser way than the Government Health Advisers would like. People also eat too much fatty food. Some people get by on a lifetime of drug taking. Many fail to exercise. However, family culture and the obvious signs of damage to lifestyle which others can see, but to which the subject may be blind, give the answer to the question. If it does matter, then make the choice to make the difference. It is not a time for pussyfooting around; it is a time for powerful and persistent action that works. You won't be popular, but you may save a life.

Tip No 72: Habits elimination
For ever!

CHAPTER SEVENTEEN

Anger management

What helps you most in managing your anger is not getting angry. If that is not possible, then removing yourself early is the next best thing. If that is not possible, then refraining from acting out the anger though violence is better than hitting people. More seriously, there are two routes to anger management: either superficial and behavioural ways of managing difficult situations or finding ways within yourself to move on from being angry so you can manage the situations in a way that is less damaging to yourself and others.

The push should, of course, come from the individual: "I don't like what happens when I get angry, I don't get what I want, I don't feel good about myself, and everybody hates me. Hmmm. What else could I do instead of throwing things around and hitting people?" Anger management has to be the choice of the individual: feelings arise (can I change how I feel?) and behaviour is exhibited in line with these feelings (can I change what I do?). Of course, coaching from others can help in clarifying the answers to these early questions and in helping the changes to happen (in both cases the answer is yes), but only if the person is willing to engage about his or her anger.

That motivation can be encouraged by those around, of course (call the police, seek payment for the broken chair, and so on).

You have to see the value in managing anger, and as much of the benefit in finding a cooler way to manage things is relational (avoiding the aftermath, for instance), there may be less perceived value for people with Asperger's than for NTs. It is also necessary to believe that it is possible to stop the red mist falling, and this may be an aspiration beyond the grasp of some Aspies.

There is also always a choice for those around to make the message clear that the behaviour associated with anger is unacceptable and that change is demanded. No matter where the motivation comes from, though, the person has to sign up to wanting to manage his or her anger.

Emotions arise and flow, washing over our experience in a constantly changing cocktail of experience. If we have insufficient love, perhaps we get lonely. If we have too much anger and we fail to find a channel for it to flow though, we get frustrated, and may explode. Anger itself is unavoidable and healthy: it gets things done and is a great agent for change. The frustration arising from unexpressed anger is a different kettle of fish, though: it indicates that the anger is not getting things done because it is not being channelled creatively.

Constipated anger explodes and produces violent, destructive behaviour, and this is what needs to be managed. There are steps in the process of moving towards explosion. Less anger coming in may be desirable (acceptance of things as they are rather than how you would like them to be). Anger expressed as it arises is healthy (assertively seeking to negotiate for a better fit lifestyle). Frustration arises only when things get blocked, and the individual is ultimately responsible for that (consequences, ownership and choice will help the process of flow; lack of them will increase constipated rage).

As with sex and drugs, it is rare to hear people explain how compelling the experience is. Raging is a wonderful idea at the time— indeed it is so good that it seems to be the only option left. People report tunnel vision and red mist and a loss of sense of self as they unload all the pressure they have been carrying around, finally saying exactly what they wanted to say all along, finally moving things forward so that the other person finally understands. Finally! The worm turns! And it feels good.

So the best time to intervene is not when the chair is about to be overturned. There may be short-term emergency strategies which can be taught and learnt to get past this moment without the kitchen being trashed. Simple agreed "time out" rules are helpful, but they need to be rehearsed and agreed in the cool of another moment. It takes a while for people to cool off (longer for men than for women by a long distance, apparently), so time out is good if it is long enough (half an hour at least), and if the agreement is to get into separate spaces but to return to the issue when everyone is calm, because anger thinks it has reason, and it wants to be heard. When rehearsing, you must agree a plan: "Either of us can call time out. If we do, then you go there, out of sight, and I go here, out of sight. We get on with our lives for at least half an hour, without coming into contact for any reason. Then we decide whether to return to the discussion." Time out is best said and signalled, hand up like a traffic cop: "Time out!" A very good strategy is for the angry one to take a walk around the block.

This is just damage limitation, however, and although it is important in the short term, it cures nothing. Displacement activities may work a bit better. Jerry used to go outside and chop firewood into very small pieces. Housework can also be useful. However, one may need to learn the signs of impending anger: at a certain point explosion is inevitable, and that explosion exerts centrifugal force. The closer you get to it, the less likely you are to be able to avoid it, so early warnings are important. They are likely to be individual, and so a useful conversation is one that enables the subject to identify early warning signs.

Consequences are useful motivators to encourage the person to consider whether it is worthwhile giving up the red mist in exchange for a more balanced communication style. Anything broken has to be paid for, for instance, and perhaps the breaker has to make the repair arrangements. Other consequences are possible to imagine too: "I hate you when you behave like that, and I want to spit in your food, so if that happens again, I am going out to a restaurant without you for dinner—you can do your own cooking."

Anger can be specific or existential. Existential anger comes when the person is pissed off with everything. Specific anger comes when a person explodes because there is no milk in the fridge. Again! "So if it matters that much to you, you be responsible for doing the milk shopping." Existential anger is harder to change, of course. The basic rule is that you are responsible for your own life no matter what. The rest of us can be around to support you, but until you decide on a direction, we are powerless to help. It all comes down to acceptance, ownership and choice.

There may be ways you can formulate your requests as an angry person, and those around can perhaps learn to interact with you in a formulaic way that enables you to hear each other. Acknowledging your feelings, making requests and allowing people to offer alternatives are all helpful. However, all this is predicated on the individual coming to terms with his or her need to manage feelings so that violence, or the threat of violence (blackmail), does not come to call. If this acknowledgement is not forthcoming, or if it does not result in action, the necessity for those around is to ensure that they are protected. Families are strong, and to exclude someone is not an easy or familiar thing to do. Many families living with Asperger's come to realise that services are clumsy, blunt instruments that sometimes feel as though they do more damage than good. However, no one is served by allowing the person with Asperger's to develop a violence habit, so police or psychiatric intervention may be the only resort, and early intervention is always better than late.

Tip No 73: Leading by demonstration
I am feeling . . .

Tip No 74: "Clevertalk"
Agree, find common ground, take them away from conflict

CHAPTER EIGHTEEN

Romance

The most desired change in most young men with Asperger's Syndrome is that they want—but cannot get (or keep)—a girl-friend. No doubt the converse is also true; I have less experience of these conversations, though what I have heard tends to tell me it is so.

A partner offers connection, intimacy and status, and perhaps to an extent a sense of completeness: we are nominally monogamous creatures, and perhaps getting the partner means that you can stop trying and enjoy feeling complete. These simple motivations seem to be identical to those held by most of the population. I am aware that sociological changes may not quite bear this monogamous world view out, though these changes may be more economic than social. It is quite simple in the end: pop down to the bar on Friday night and watch them all flirting away. People like the opposite sex, and try to "get off" with them. There is a common pattern here for certain: people want partners. Growing up with Asperger's must attack your confidence, and in fact the inherent perceptual deficits that arise out of the neural architecture probably do mean that flirting is a difficult thing to learn: it is one of the most responsive and unpredictable conversational and behavioural games to play.

However, it can be done, and I know of some people with Asperger's who are married (many to NTs) and settled, with children. Of course all the other problems do not go away, and new ones can arrive specifically within the relationship.

Probably people with Asperger's have already experienced an inability (or perceived it as failure) and felt that they were left aside, not considered in the great mating game, before they even leave school. Without the usual quotient of willingness to party, they are disadvantaged by not putting themselves into the usual flirting arenas.

Some people with Asperger's are likely to be gay. I have yet to meet one who has shared this with me, but we must assume it is so, and the immediate extra problem I can imagine is that of initially coming out as an idiosyncratic and different sort of person. When this is achieved, the problems are much the same: making contact with suitable people and going though the necessary moves that will give you both space to make the choice of whether to go further or not.

However, it is not necessary to go to loud clubs and gigs, nor to drink too much and do the pub thing, in order to meet people. For every quiet and unclubbable man out there, I am prepared to believe there is a woman who would value the unpretentious honesty and vulnerability which also goes with the condition. I often suggest that my clients go and have a look at people in the streets and see how many physically imperfect specimens have found a partner: it is not physical perfection that guarantees you a girl (or bloke). It is much more a problem of getting past the first post and actually meeting people of the opposite sex. Only by meeting people can you find that needle in the haystack. Of course agencies, speed dating and adverts might well work, as they do give you a way to get past stage one.

Stage two is moving past the first half hour towards a situation in which both people want to spend an hour or two together. A practical point that comes up sometimes is that the man in particular has to have a repertoire of suitable activities: managing pub behaviour, finding a place with live music that isn't too sticky, getting cinema tickets, ordering in a restaurant, and so on—all these may have to be learnt. Chatting is also a skill, and there may be a certain inhibition in chatting to a woman who may or may not turn into a girlfriend: performance anxiety.

"Would you care for a cup of coffee?" is a euphemism if ever there was one. We hope that sometime they get into the same space: my place or yours? Does either one of them know what they are doing? It is quite likely that neither of them will have any experience.

I took a couple of clients through a sex education film. We discussed condoms, STDs and technique as well as communication, including saying no and responding to no. It was all very academic and quiet, so I showed them Michael Winterbottom's film *9 Songs*. This is a completely explicit film of a sexual relationship between two people, and is almost entirely taken up with bed scenes in which the entirety of their sexual experience is shown on screen. I chose this film because it is a good attempt at showing a sexual relationship in a real way, and is so different to any porn films. Both clients had seen porn films, and I wanted them to see technique in terms of what people do with each other, roughly speaking. Bernard, who had visited a prostitute in the past, sat through the whole thing, and at the end his comment was: "There's a great deal of foreplay, isn't there?" The other thing both of them said immediately was: "Right. How do we get from here to there?" At least they have a few more ideas than they had—foreplay can last more than three minutes, for instance.

Flirting is a specific subset of social skills which is not often taught to this population. It is best done unconsciously and is therefore almost impossible to teach by simulation. I have been to the pubs and cafés here, with these same clients, looking for flirting couples, and they hide from us when they see us coming (with the video camera). Flirting is best done with a couple of drinks, in a fun atmosphere, with no pressure, in the company of a small group of not so close friends. Which is asking the Aspie to pass though the eye of a needle: the setting is wrong for him and is likely to create the pressure that will prevent the flow.

I often suggest that clients join clubs and groups, a good strategy because it gives you common ground, something you can share, as well as introductions to a group of people, some of whom will be of the opposite sex.

Some parents will be worried. Some sons or daughters will not share their experiences, and some will not get to the point where they are ready to try and meet people. Parental fears are real, of course: pregnancy would not be good, nor would disease. Entering into a sexual relationship is a process of showing that you are ready to swim in deeper waters, and there are sharks out there. The downside to a loving relationship is the emotional hurt, and if your son or daughter is vulnerable and a little fragile, it can be difficult to watch them open themselves up to heartbreak.

Then there is the conduct of the relationship itself: She gives him all her money! He always has to make the journey! They just sit around all day! Now I'm doing her washing as well! I think they're using drugs! She wraps him round her little finger!

Parents have to allow this to happen—if it is going to happen, then they will not able to stop it, so the best thing is to move into an advisory position as soon as possible, whilst maintaining whatever boundaries and expectations are felt to be correct in the family.

Then there is the break-up, which may cause depression and a real unwillingness to get out there again. Promiscuity is more accepted in men than in women, and there may be an unusual attitude in some women who see sex in a more functional way than us complicated NTs, wanting to have the experience without the attachments (what are those attachments anyway?). Does it matter?

CHAPTER NINETEEN

Money

Money is the easiest and the hardest. Having no intrinsic value of its own, it reflects one's feelings about oneself very clearly. In the context of the clients I have worked with, there is a complete spectrum from people having no control over their money whatsoever, either spending it all or letting their parents manage it with no sense of ownership, to people with complete control, who either let no money out of their control or keep their financial situation entirely secret, apparently coping fine. I have also met those in the middle, who just pay their bills as they arrive and give themselves a reasonable allowance which they can spend on whatever they choose. In the context of the families I have met, some have a distant control by maintaining complete access to their son's accounts, checking on a weekly basis. Others just pay all the bills, allowing the son to keep all his income. A few just seem to leave him to it. However, money discussions can easily be sabotaged by hot emotion, as can many other important topics.

Tip No 75: More "Clevertalk"
The same words . . .

I once met two people in the same week: both earned the same money, and both were dead drunk and ready to spill the beans. This was in the eighties, when big cheques were the order of the day for the lucky ones. They were both earning the equivalent of a quarter of a million a year. One was puzzled about what to do with his money. He had left his wife, given her the farmhouse they lived in, and bought himself another. He had part shares in a factory in Wales, which he had never seen, and was deeply unhappy. More money than he knew what to do with. The other, equally unhappy, just said " 'Ere. No matter how much you earn in a year, you always owe the same amount, eh?" Money does not buy happiness, apparently. Both lived alone, both were in their thirties, both were out of control, and neither was happy.

If the person with Asperger's is not handling money correctly (i.e. matching his expenditure to his income, paying a fair share of all living costs, and keeping a little Micawberish bit aside) he needs instruction. The nature of that instruction is in the coaching tips, and the rules are clear with money, as they are nowhere else in this book. It either adds up or it doesn't. You either take your responsibility or you don't. If a family colludes with a young Aspie and "lets him off" his fair share, it disempowers him, taking away his freedom to learn responsibility. If a family is doing that, it is probably because the parents have not yet come to terms with the disability and are still trying to protect the "child" from real life and keeping him as a child.

Money is the easiest in that you can play consequences very easily. This is best initiated when the child is just beginning to earn and before he gets an erroneous view of his special position (all my income is mine to save or spend on drink, pornography, and so on). The only way you learn that bills have to be paid and that income has to remain larger than expenditure, no matter what, is to have the experience of running out of money and not being able to do what you want.

Money is the hardest because it is so linked with emotion, and the instinct to protect and be powerful is so strong. Giving in to this is designed to make you feel good, not to help the younger person learn and grow, and keeps him dependent by stealing away his power.

I know of two people with Asperger's. Both have the same disposable income. One lives alone, in his own flat, rent and council tax paid by the benefits system. He pays all his bills by standing order, and gives himself an allowance of spending money which is transferred to a separate account. He draws this out whenever he wants, but manages to keep his average drawings a little less than his average transfer, so this account slowly accrues a surplus, currently standing at nearly a thousand pounds. His other account receives his income, pays all his standing orders and direct debits, and transfers his weekly allowance to his cash machine account. This is also arranged so that outgoings are, on average, smaller than incomings, and the balance currently stands at fifteen hundred pounds. If he wants to go to the seaside, buy a CD, or go to a restaurant, he can. He never worries about money.

The other receives all his income into one account, has his rent and council tax paid by the benefit system just like the previous person, draws cash when he feels like it, and signs mobile phone contracts regularly because it makes him feel powerful. He trades phones and other techno stuff on eBay, often making a profit which he turns straight into cash. He rarely has enough money to pay bills, and regularly has to ask his parents for a loan to pay the gas or electricity bill. He worries about money all the time, and often has to ask his parents to negotiate his way out of a loan or phone account. His credit rating is terrible, so if he ever needed a mortgage, he would not get one. The first person has a perfect credit rating.

As with all things, if the person is not seeing the picture in a healthy way, it is for the family to bring him up to date, possibly by Tough Love techniques, certainly using consequences. Sometimes it is hard to say no, even though it is clear that acquiescing yet again is no more than collusion in a game designed to let him off the responsibility hook. Who gets to feel good and who gets to feel bad?

CHAPTER TWENTY

Family bonds: parents' experiences

L iving with Asperger's is uncharted territory. No matter how many times you read this book, you will still be unsure what you should do next.

Many fathers leave the family. Others bury themselves in work and hand over parenting to the mother. Brothers and sisters very often feel overlooked, ignored and undervalued. Mothers can become traditional, co-dependent, overprotective and bitterly angry, able to bring social workers to their knees with a look. Yet the family is the strongest unit of support, and people with Asperger's tend to look to the stereotype to measure their normality, and attach themselves eagerly to the ongoing family pattern, sometimes becoming reluctant to let go.

Tip No 76: Moving beyond co-dependence
Get support and move forward

The realisation that your child has Asperger's often only comes gradually. The state of play in terms of professional understanding varies greatly, and a formal diagnosis may or may not arrive in childhood, or at all.

The point of contact with all services is the GP, who is unlikely to know about Asperger's and is likely to be an obstacle rather than an enabler. Budgets are tight, and there is none for Asperger's in any case. Getting a diagnosis often relies on the family pushing past the GP, perhaps finding the information themselves (giving a social imbalance to the entire scene, of course, as those with a better education generally push more effectively), but perhaps being supported by medical or education professionals. Getting an accurate, believable, high status diagnosis can involve several thousand pounds and a long waiting list, but it is an essential tool in fighting for appropriate support, especially in the education system, where there is at least a commitment to providing an appropriate and accessible curriculum for each individual child and meeting any special needs that obscure this target. GPs respond well to information, pressure and continued consistency. They respond much worse to combat, retreating and defending very efficiently.

Parents have to learn the single most effective tool in their armoury of weapons to use in order to obtain the best chance for their child. That weapon is called "Making a Fuss", and it is a multi-task weapon in that the same procedure works at all levels.

- Follow procedures rapidly. Always ask for the next step in advance (If this is unsuccessful, what do I do next? Can I appeal?).
- Get communication in writing. If it comes verbally, make notes and send them to the other person with an invitation to amend them. Keep them in a chronological file, and keep a brief diary so you can see and explain how time is moving forward.
- Prepare your case and stick to your guns. Avoid outright shouting if you can, but do it if you need to. Have a clear request at every turn (I want to be referred to a consultant).
- Outflank the procedure by appeals to politicians: everyone has a political boss. Health authorities have Trust members, you have MPs and local councillors, social workers and teachers have chairs of social services or education committees. Let them know what is happening as early as you like, and complain, even if you are not quite sure you have a fair case.

- Seek help at meetings: you are entitled to it and there are people who will not need money from you in order to offer their services.
- Keep notes of every promise made and seek time frames (You will send me the notes of the meeting? When can I expect them?).
- Reveal your emotion: it is for the professionals to manage the individual's emotional demands and to make the difficult decisions. They will try to engage you in that balancing process because they feel uncomfortable with it themselves. Avoid this. Your role is to get the best for your child. Shout and weep and refuse to accept anything you don't feel comfortable with.
- Be reasonable. In contrast to the above, you also have to listen to the professionals, because they know a lot more and have a much more widely based knowledge than you, and they may be right.
- Never give up. When you are headline news in the national papers it may be time to rethink your ambitions, but not before. This is an unfair world, especially for the unbudgeted Aspies. So make your demands. In that way the pressure for a budget to be created is increased.

In the midst of what I unfortunately but necessarily characterise as a "battle", the diagnosis is made and the news shared. I have no direct experience myself of what it must be like to hear that your child can be described with a short label and long explanation of the syndrome, but I do have children, and can only imagine how difficult, disappointing, frustrating, hurtful and scary it must be. Almost all of this book is in some way connected with the notion of coming to terms with this. In order to come to terms with a diagnosis you need information, and you need to go through a process (probably something like this: denial, anger, depression, bargaining, negation, acceptance) in order to feel whole again. Much easier to do that by talking than by losing yourself in frenetic activity (part of the denial stage).

Of course, diagnosis only happens if the people in most contact with the child notice a problem and call attention to it. This attention may come from teachers at nursery school, or even from health visitors and paediatric staff (though it is probable that parents will have to seek the attention). There is a natural and completely healthy tendency to give the child room to leave old habits behind and to teach him new and better ways to manage his life without the major disruption of entering the Special Needs world. Whilst this may slow things down a little, that is a judgement which can only be made with hindsight. At the time, when a child first mixes with others, there is a socialisation process which is led by teachers, with support from non-teaching and medical staff where necessary, and in my experience children are usually given space to find their feet and to learn to manage themselves in a positive and loving way.

> *An inspector watches a class of special needs children involved in a group activity. A child wanders off away from the activity, and is returned by a teaching assistant. Things go along. The same child wanders away again. The teaching assistant takes the child's hand and leads her out of the room as she begins a tantrum.*
>
> *Later, the inspector asks why the teaching assistant did that: was there no sense of the teacher being in control? What happened? Why was this child marked out in this way? Why was she going into a tantrum?*
>
> *The teacher explains: "This child has a very short attention span, and when she goes off task she becomes disruptive. Our strategy—have a copy—is to remove her on the second time, as we know that the bad experience of her throwing a tantrum in the classroom disrupts the other children and upsets her badly. I raised an eyebrow—perhaps you didn't notice—which is the prearranged signal for my assistant to take the step to move her out of the classroom. We have a set of learning activities for her to use at these times."*
>
> *There is a law which requires that the curriculum must be differentiated to meet the needs of the individual. Sometimes the most important step to accessing the school curriculum is managing to stay on an emotionally even keel. Teachers need to make sure they support this by allowing the child to experience continued calmness.*

Those with autism may well be spotted much earlier than those with Asperger's, and the latter may not be spotted for a long time because their intelligence and verbal ability, combined with their choice to manage problems in a passive way, can work to extend the teacher's patience and support which arise from her professional and personal hope that any problems will remain manageable. At some indefinable point this can become unhealthy, as the child is likely to be in an environment which is increasingly uncomfortable for him and in which he is seriously underperforming. Also, problems arising from the frustration inherent in this are likely to be exhibited at home more than at school, and this difference, not so much in perception as in actual behaviour, can begin to drive a wedge between the parents and the school, damaging trust on the way.

Schools in the UK, under pressure to perform and include, seemingly tend to overestimate their own expertise at the expense of the child's experience. Tribunals, the last port of call in the battle to be offered an appropriate education, have 25% of their time taken up by struggles to find the right place for ASD pupils. This reflects parental experience—it is a long and difficult road to a tribunal, with many frustrations and hindrances on the way.

Every child has a right to an appropriate education. Nowadays the hot education concept is to differentiate the curriculum in order to make sure each individual can access it despite any specific needs.

Midge was thirteen, attending a new school, in the eldest year as the school grew up with its first intake. He threw major tantrums when things didn't go right, felt that he was ostracised, and was in major trouble at school. I observed him for a day. The other "naughty boys", with whom he chose to sit, distracted him continually. Almost all the teachers he saw in a day only noticed him when he was out of line. None checked his work, few sat down with him. The level of his work, apart from always being about football no matter what subject he as in, was way below his capabilities, and he spent maybe 15% of his time "on task", using the rest of it to laugh and joke and mess about.

I suggested that each session was begun by the teacher noting him by name and telling him where to sit (near to the front, away from the "naughty boys"), and that each teacher looked at his work before he left the room and gave him immediate feedback. The school could not do that, and he soon left, entering Special Education at enormous cost.

In the UK, the mechanism is to prepare a Statement of Special Educational Needs (a Statement). Parents can be deeply involved in this process, and have considerable power in agreeing the content. When that Statement is written (or if it is not), sometimes the family has to help the school do better. This might even mean teaching the teachers—it is always difficult to teach a professional, but sometimes the parents do actually know better. However, the point of school is to socialise the child, and the essential part of this is to support the child in learning to wait, share, mix with and operate in a group, and if she or he can learn this, it will be the most valuable lesson for later life.

I have mentioned in the text above how parents are programmed for their children to fly the nest. When they fail to do so, or teeter on the edge for a long time, parents are faced with the thought that lifetime dependency may be about to begin. This is usually hard to talk about, as all options can seem to be unattractive or unattainable at this point, and an attractive (but futile) strategy is to ignore the problem for a long time, hoping it will go away. Whilst it may well go away simply because people with Asperger's are slower to develop than the NTs, it may not; and a period of ignoring it may allow things to develop to a point of no return as dependency becomes entrenched.

When the child leaves school, less attention is paid to the special needs of the individual. In the UK, it may be that she or he is entitled to benefits: Disability Living Allowance or Incapacity Benefit often comes to people with Asperger's in my experience. It is of course a bureaucratic process to get them, but people do. However, this is not necessarily the best choice for someone who is teetering on the edge of the nest. Exams may have been overlooked; they can be picked up on at college, where the social scene is less malevolent. Those teetering in the other direction may need support right there and then as the pressures of the adult world, with its lack of structure and competitive nature, hit them. Some may go to university and be well supported there, protected for a further three years, though there is a pattern of some breaking down in the mid-course. Some will get a job. Some will keep that job; others will find long-term employment too tricky to achieve. Some may get girl- or boyfriends and find ways to make that work, and of course some will fail while others will succeed.

Over the period from leaving school to the end of their twenties, the teeterers will probably fall one way or the other. Parents will watch nervously, intervening as they feel is right, reading and re-reading this book every morning, of course. Gradually the future outlines itself as the years flow along, and the next crucially important question comes up: who will be there when I am gone? This is the question that started the National Autistic Society (NAS) in the early 1960s, giving rise to one of the world's most important and influential organisations for people with ASD. The NAS has made a monumental difference to the life chances of autistic people everywhere, including Aspies, but they have no catch-all remit that would guarantee a good support service for each individual. The influence is there in the level of knowledge and various examples of best practice, but it is for each individual family to find their niche. All I want to say here is that the question demands some serious consideration well in advance.

CHAPTER TWENTY-ONE

Special interests

A feature of this condition is rigidity of thought: this can sometimes present itself as an overwhelming interest in a narrow topic. Some might call this an obsession, and sometimes people with Asperger's syndrome do indeed develop obsessive-compulsive habits. Some also develop habits which can be seen in a negative light, whilst others can develop overly strong habits of cleanliness or social conduct.

I know one young woman who knows everything about Pink Floyd. This is harmless, I think, though I now know considerably more than I used to about this excellent band. (I know they are excellent, as I have had to re-listen to the records! Anyway, I saw them play in Syd Barrett's day.)

I know another who has felt a need to collect all the available records of various people (Elvis, Nick Drake and others). This is difficult in that he has sometimes chosen to buy rather than budget, and those old LPs take up a lot of space. However, eBay beckons, and he has a lot of value in this collection.

A young man with semantic pragmatic disorder (too complicated a label for him to be able remember) is writing a novel focused around a computer game of choice in order to get in practice for writing a big *Lord of the Rings*-type fantasy trilogy.

Another is writing a sci-fi film script and starting a film club for showing rare sci-fi films and shorts.

I just keep on writing songs and playing my guitar. The only difference is that I also have work and relationship arenas in my life. If the interest is getting in the way of other life, consequences are there to be experienced, and coaching is there to help the person to broaden his awareness. If it seems he is hiding behind the interest, then create good reasons for him to come out a bit. If it is unhealthy, exert parental force if that is possible. It seems to me that having a strong interest that you can use to explore your abilities is a good thing, and that those around you can bring you down to earth by use of some of these coaching tips if it is going too far. I realise that this can be a major task, and I suppose I am presenting the alternative view that maybe "obsessional interests" are just interests which have become a little too strong because of the paucity of other things in one's life.

PART IV

APPENDICES

Information sheet

This is information I prepared for people with no prior knowledge of Asperger's syndrome. A brief introduction is followed by some notes on the features often associated with the Triad of Impairments, with an outline of some of the basic observable behaviour and some suggestions as to the reactions you may have. It may be useful to note your reactions— they sometimes tell you as much as anything else. I have included a number of simple suggested strategies as well as information about the sub-groups and some age-specific notes.

About Asperger's

Asperger's is a developmental disorder, present from birth and before, affecting the entirety of a person's experience as he or she grows. New research suggest 0.6% incidence, affecting about ten males to one female. It is diagnosed though observation of behaviour and discussion of history. Asperger's is an autistic spectrum disorder, differentiated from autism by normal intelligence (often high) and normal syntax (grammatical speech production). To be diagnosed, overall behaviour needs to reflect the Triad of Impairments, which outlines difficulties in three areas (see below). Diagnosis is made on the overall pattern; not all these features will be present in any one individual. Many people are not diagnosed, so it may be good to give them the benefit of the doubt.

Triad of Impairments: communication

Behavioural habits

- Talking off the subject
- Bending the topic to fit the thinking
- Low responsiveness
- Flat voice
- Unable to read emotion from another's face
- Limited facial expression
- Poor eye contact (especially reciprocal)
- Doesn't look at others
- Watches mouth, not face
- Little gesture
- Comes too close
- Talks too little or too much
- Incoherent conversation
- Idiosyncratic use of words
- Repetitive patterns of speech

Look out for your reaction

- Not following
- Beginning to feel trapped
- Something odd here!
- Poor rhythm: long pauses or interrupting
- Feeling protective
- Feeling invaded (walking backwards!)
- We're going round in circles!
- Wanting to end the conversation

Useful strategies

- Relax and give him/her time

- Talk slowly and clearly
- Repeat yourself in the simplest way possible
- Check if s/he understands
- Draw a mind map or flow diagram of the conversation
- Write action points down
- Summarise and tell him/her that you are moving on to the next point
- Give warning about time running out
- Stick to boundaries

Triad of Impairments: social relationships

Behavioural habits

- Lonely (not interested in friends, a loner, avoids others, no friends)
- Isolated (spends the day alone, either going for a walk or staying in, often using computers)
- Doesn't easily use public transport, shops, etc.
- Overly dependent on parents
- Functional approach to relationships (only contacts others to have his/her needs met)
- Something feels odd (clumsy social approach that leaves you feeling something isn't quite right)
- Fixated on a person (especially the stereotypical blonde young woman!)
- Shy
- Passive
- Detached (weak "theory of mind" leads to lack of normal awareness of experience, viewpoint and feelings of others)
- One-sided approach (how come we always end up talking about you?)

Look out for your reaction

- Bored
- Wishing that something could be done
- Interested in his/her abilities
- Uncomfortable

- Frustrated
- Puzzled
- Feeling overly responsible

Useful strategies

- Be interested
- Name his/her feelings
- Check whether s/he feels comfortable and whether something could help (change rooms, move seats, etc.)
- Interrupt and bring the conversation back to where it needs to be
- Tell him/her what you or others may be experiencing
- Manage yourself so as to reduce stress (sit back, look away, wait, relax)

Triad of Impairments: rigid thinking

Behavioural habits

- "Goes on"
- Resistant to change
- Narrow interests
- Unwilling to try
- Obsessive or compulsive or both (obsession can perhaps be controlled: think of it as an extreme interest; compulsion can be very hard to control: it is not a source of pleasure to the person and probably needs to be allowed space)
- Very knowledgeable about certain interests (may have qualifications to degree level or above, and may be very willing and able to talk about certain interests and thoughts)
- Poor at making or enacting plans
- Repetitive routines

Look out for your reaction

- Helpless
- Frustrated

- Wanting to move on
- Impatient
- Amused or puzzled

Useful strategies

- You may have to ask them to stop talking about something: be kind but blunt and keep to the rule. Enjoying their adherence to their subject but not colluding with it helps to make it easier to manage. Be very clear about the purpose of the conversation; remind and ask them how the divergence to a narrow interest can help you to achieve your goal. Spend some time talking about the chosen topic, as it will help them to relax and feel valued. State overtly that this has to be limited to maybe ten minutes, and really join in the conversation for that time.
- Check if plans are within his or her competence (Can you do that? Will you do that?).
- Allow routines to run their course as they may well be essential.

Additional difficulties: perception

Features

- Sensitive to noise, light, and stimulation (individuals may have a strong awareness of background stimuli and find it hard to blot them out in order to concentrate)
- Distractable (focus may be hard to achieve)
- Fascinated with certain objects (fascination can be as strong as compulsion, or it can be a real source of pleasure and exploration)
- Afraid (fear often arises from apparently small causes; however, it is always real at the time)

Look out for your reaction

- Not understanding
- Impatient
- Unsympathetic

Useful strategies

- Ask and make the necessary adjustments
- Allow time

Additional difficulties: life experience

Features

- Anger
- Depression
- Hopelessness

The experience of living with this condition and trying to make things happen whilst feeling excluded and lonely can lead to learnt feelings of fear, anger, depression, and so on, as it would with anyone else.

Look out for your reaction

- Not understanding
- Impatient

Useful strategies

As you would for any other person: manage any risk, establish rapport and present possibilities

Sub-groups: aloof

Over-formal, stilted, isolated, perhaps electively mute, distant, withdrawn, perhaps not caring for self and hence dishevelled, odorous, noticeable

Look out for your reaction

- Not understanding
- Impatient

Useful strategies

- Relax and accept
- They have been told before how difficult they make it for themselves: don't bother to nag!

Sub-groups: active but odd

Own needs the priority, not willing to share, no concept of consensus or negotiation, rules or norms; deficits in non-verbal communication, complex language and abstract concepts

Look out for your reaction

- Not understanding
- Impatient

Useful strategies

- Be clear about boundaries
- Explain consequences
- Be very blunt about possible future experiences (these people can easily end up in court, jail or hospital)
- Use visuals to help them understand (pictures, social stories, flow diagrams, notes, mind maps)

Sub-groups: passive

Accepting of but indifferent to approaches, compliant, vulnerable, might enjoy people but make no moves, change and stress difficult to manage. It may be that these are the people who have the most potential and fewest sabotage strategies, and hence are the most likely to achieve independence.

Look out for your reaction

- Not understanding
- Impatient

Useful strategies

- Listen
- Make suggestions
- Check how they are feeling
- Explain simple things to them (e.g. your turn to buy the coffee)
- Take time
- Lead them into managing more at their own pace

Relationships with families

Features

- Over-protective parents
- One or both parents similarly affected
- Untrusting

Relationships with families may be unusual. There is a strong heritability of this condition and a low historical rate of diagnosis: it is quite likely, therefore, that either parent (or both) may have this condition themselves, in which case they need these strategies to be used sympathetically, as they will probably not recognise the condition in themselves, nor will they have been treated or supported in managing it.

Look out for your reaction

- Not understanding
- Impatient
- Wanting the person to have his or her own voice

Useful strategies

- Accept that the parents are there because they do not believe their son or daughter will get a fair deal otherwise
- Be clear about what is possible and what is not
- Under-promise and over-deliver
- Use any of these strategies if they help
- Seek to understand the parents' point of view

Co-morbidity

Other conditions quite frequently arise in conjunction with Asperger's syndrome, for instance:

- Dyslexia
- Dysphasia
- Dyspraxia
- Schizophrenia
- Clumsiness
- Psychosis
- Anxiety
- Depression
- Drug and alcohol abuse

Sometimes it happens that people get involved in drugs and alcohol, and they might find it very hard to control, either lapsing into addiction or overusing drugs (especially cannabis) to the point of psychosis. They can also be very vulnerable to drug dealers, mistaking the process as one of friendship.

Look out for your reaction

- Not understanding
- Impatient
- Not believing

Useful strategies

Seek to find out what they find easy and what they find hard: be a detective rather than a stranger. Ask them how they would like things to be done: they may not want a cup of tea for fear of spilling it, and may find it hard to read or to take notes. Unusual features may include an inability to recognise faces, or reliance on sameness of clothes in order to recognise you. Window blinds may need to be drawn, and so on: you need to make space for them to tell you what will make them comfortable. Remember that they may well be very shy and embarrassed.

Some age-specific notes

Some indicators at age 0–6

- Slow to develop language? Extraordinarily adult language structure? Doesn't listen?
- Repetitive play?
- Laughs at his own thoughts?
- Stays away from peers?
- Watches the same DVDs repeatedly?
- Picky eater?
- Marked preferences for certain clothes?
- Doesn't like noisy places?
- Tantrums, continuing for longer than usual?

Some indicators at age 6–11

- Very good at some subjects at school (especially maths or music)?
- Difficult when he comes home from school?
- Weekend routine very strong?
- Stays up in his bedroom too much?
- Argues with siblings?
- Few friends?
- Friends with the local bully or the local outcast?
- Resists going to school?
- Doesn't enjoy playtimes?
- Not into team games?

Some indicators at age 11–17

- Excluded from social groups?
- Barrack-room lawyer?
- Untidy or chaotic?
- Bullied?
- Dropping out of school?
- No girlfriends?
- Doesn't take responsibility for money, food, etc?
- Frightened?

- Develops rigid habits?
- Knows everything about something?
- Repetitive conversations?
- Worried parents?
- Music, clothes, etc. mark him out as being too much into a style?
- Drugs, alcohol, exercise, computer games etc. taking over?
- Too much time alone?
- Aggressive?
- Paranoid?

Some indicators at age 17–25

- Friends move on and leave him behind?
- Slow to move out?
- Succession of failures (jobs lost, courses not completed, etc)?
- Doesn't complete the growing up process?
- Depression?
- Isolation?
- Dependent behaviour with drugs, alcohol, money, food, domestic tasks?
- Recognisably odd?
- People start to compensate (friends sometimes "take him out")?
- Focus on what he will do (but not yet)?
- Loses routine?
- Lonely?
- Criminal?
- Uses pornography?
- Develops chaotic lifestyle?

Some indicators at age 25+

- Increasingly isolated?
- Anger turns to depression?
- Habits start to set?
- Poor self-care?
- Job below his capabilities?
- Doesn't do much?

- Asks parents, family or the state for too much?
- Gullible?
- Dodgy friends?

Coaching fundamentals

There are four NLP principles behind all this work, which are very helpful, and which you need to keep in your mind whilst using all the coaching tips. This is the basic operating manual for coaching.

- Well formed outcome
- Rapport
- Behavioural flexibility
- Sensory acuity

Also worth putting into the mix are two helpful models for intervention which also arise out of NLP: the TOTE model and the Basic Intervention model, and a helpful tool for change called Logical Levels.

Well formed outcome

The very best coaching question to ask is "What do you want?" There is always an answer, though sometimes it will be a soft answer (I want to feel satisfied) and other times it will be harder (I want to have enough money).

Of course you can play with time frames: What do you want right now? What do you want to have done by the time you are an old man on your deathbed? What do you want to change in the next year? You can also chunk up (What do you want that for? What sort of life will that give you? What's good about that?), and chunk down (Exactly what will that be like? When? Exactly how much money is enough?).

An ambition which you have worked through so that it can be defined as completely desirable, with no part of you objecting, is well formed. Here is a nine-point matrix for working out exactly what it is that you want:

1. State positively and specifically what you want. (Not "I want to lose weight" but "I want to weigh ten stone". Not "I want to give up smoking" but "I want to breathe freely". Not "I am lonely" but "I want a circle of ten friends whom I see at least every month". Not "I want to get out of debt" but "I want to be financially secure".)

2. What specific sensory evidence will you see, hear, feel smell, taste when you have your ambition? (My jeans will fall down! I will be able to run for the bus without panting. I will have £2000 on my bank statement. I will get emails.)

3. Is it in your control? There is no point in having a well formed outcome for someone else—adjust it until it is all in your control. Those friends will only come to you if you do something yourself. What can you do about it? This may in fact redefine your goal (not "I want to sell more books than J.K. Rowling" but "I want to write a book which the people I ask say is better than Harry Potter").

4. What do you lose by achieving this goal? Everything you do is done for a reason, so there will be a loss if you make a change: you will have to buy more clothes, eat less food, give up pasta, lose contact with your work smoking club outside the back door, lose your ability to plan your day without thinking, and your privacy to an extent. You may have to spend less, or carry less cash in your wallet. If these things matter, you may want to adopt a plan which will give you what you are losing in a different way ("I never go out on Monday or Tuesday nights" or "I will give up my mobile phone contract in order to have more cash in my pocket").

5. What is the context of this? When, where and with whom do you want this?
6. Is it worth the time?
7. Is it worth the cost?
8. Is it worth the effort?
9. Is it something you can imagine yourself doing or having? Is it you?

Work through all these questions, adjusting your definition of what you want until you feel completely happy with the outcome, then stick with it until you have good reason to change.

Rapport

Rapport is being in tune with the other person—something people with Asperger's find very hard to achieve but we NTs do so well that we hardly know how it works. Lack of rapport can render a person unable to speak; excess of rapport can lead to agreement with all sorts of nefarious undertakings.

In essence, in order to create rapport, you match the other person's rhythms. Sometimes this is about mirroring their posture, gesture, speech (use of words, speaking rhythm, voice tonality, and so on). So long as you are subtle, they will notice you doing this and will relax, so that it is possible to lead them forward to where you want just by gently demonstrating.

- Listen
- Answer (without interrupting) to the point of what was said before, going on to what you want to say
- Watch their responses very closely; notice all signs of discomfort, disagreement or non-acceptance and deal with the point before going forward
- Create nil pressure—nothing is expected, silence or talk is all OK, neither of you is in charge; be very present
- Match posture (sit if they do, lean forward, legs crossed, etc.)
- Mirror gesture in a quiet, unnoticeable way
- Start your responses with "Yes, and" rather than "No, but"
- Match their breathing rhythm
- Enter into their being so you are tuned to their wavelength

Behavioural flexibility

The basic thought that drives this principle is this: if you always do what you always did, you'll always get what you always got. If you are coaching someone and trying to promote change, and if what you are doing isn't working as well as you want, have some more tricks up your sleeve! That is why we learn new skills, techniques and disciplines, and attend conferences—to learn new tricks.

This is a random and partial list, as behavioural flexibility necessarily creates an endless collection of things that come to mind in a specific set of circumstances.

- Change the circumstances—go for a walk instead of sitting talking
- Change the subject in order to change the emotional temperature—you can go back to what you were talking about any time
- Crack a joke
- Have a cup of tea
- Sit quietly
- Change sides so you are exploring an opposite view

Sensory acuity

You have five (or perhaps six) senses: all your information comes through them, so if you can't see, hear, feel, taste or smell something, it isn't there. However, when you are working with a subject, watch closely, listen closely, attend to your own feelings—the subject is likely to have similar ones—and collect all the information you can. With close attention you can notice very subtle signs of acceptance, rejection, or building rapport. Assume that everything that you see, hear and feel is significant.

TOTE

This is a very simple structure which you can use minute by minute in a coaching session (or in life): Test-Operate-Test-Exit. Remember that the ambition in coaching is to enable change in state, cognition or behaviour, and that all behaviour means something. Establish a sense of direction.

- Test the subject's current state ("Do you understand?" "Ummm . . .")
- Operate ("Let me explain it again . . .")
- Test ("Do you understand?" "Oh yes, now I get it!")
- Exit and move on to the next point.

The whole thing can be non-verbal, of course:

- You lean back, relax and prepare to start talking about some sensitive topic, observing the subject. The subject leans forward, stuttering about something inconsequential, clearly anxious (TEST).
- You lean forward, crack a joke, establish rapport, lean back slowly in silence (OPERATE).
- The subject laughs, leans slowly back and takes a deep breath, letting it out slowly. You notice and take it as a sign of relaxation, say "Ummm . . . ?" The subject looks at you and nods a little (TEST).
- You move on to the sensitive subject (EXIT).

Basic intervention model

This is a model of a good intervention for creating change, particularly focusing on the power of the imagination.

- Establish rapport and maintain it throughout, of course
- Gather information about what the subject wants and what the story is
- Establish the required outcome (see well formed outcome above)
- Access the required resources by identifying them clearly and using the subject's own experience to recreate the required resources
- Help the person re-experience a positive moment in his history in order to recreate that feeling, so he can use it to achieve the goal whilst feeling resourceful
- Future pace by leading the subject to imagine how life will be when she or he has succeeded
- Test by exploring the subject's feelings about this goal
- Exit when you are sure you have done the job

Logical levels

This is another useful model to keep in mind. In this model there are seven levels of experience: environment, behaviour, capability, beliefs and values, identity and spirit. There is strength when there is congruity on all these levels, so if planned action comes from a strong sense of being connected and in the right place, being the right person, who believes in the goal, is definitely able to do what is required, and has done it before in the same circumstances, for instance, you may feel that it is worth putting money on. However, if another planned action is disconnected and selfish, feels wrong and is not something that anyone cares much about, nor is there anyone who feels able to do what is required or has done it before, or ever seen it done, you may not choose to put a bet on a successful outcome.

To make easy change, then, it can be represented as environmental, or at that end of the levels (think how easily most smokers accept that they may not smoke in someone's house). If you want a piece of behaviour to be strongly lodged, it needs to be placed at the identity end (think of asking a smoker to become a non-smoker, or someone who was caught speeding considering themselves to be a criminal).

Coaching tips

lways bearing the above in mind, this is a list of things I have tried and found some success with.

Tip No 1: Tell them what is required
Explain in advance, in detail and in Technicolor

The best presupposition to work with is that people say what they mean. Many of us (particularly NTs) spend a lot of energy interpreting. Sometimes it is better to explain the obvious than to let it pass unnoticed. Explaining is often welcome, and if it is an obvious point, that leads naturally to an exploration of how to respond to this information. People with Asperger's sometimes overlook or fail to receive information that we NTs take for granted, so explanations about personal space, eye contact, the need to answer questions as they are asked, and so on, may be welcome. It is helpful to mention what they will see, hear, feel, smell and taste, so they are prepared for the experience.

Tip No 2: Set up escape routes from social situations
If a person knows he can get away if it all gets too hard, he will be stronger

Large group activities (pub visits, parties, dinner parties etc.) can be stressful. Stress reduces the ability to think creatively. It may be useful to prepare someone by planning a way out which they can use at any point when they cease to enjoy the experience, such as a visit to the toilet or an early exit—give them the script if necessary ("I am so sorry but I have to go now").

Tip No 3: Listen to the end of a speech before interrupting
It is empowering to be heard in full

Many people with Asperger's have a lot to say. I found that one client would talk for fifteen minutes on one question, and it was only right at the end that I started to understand how what he said all fitted together. Many of them must experience being interrupted on a regular basis—it may be a new and welcome experience for them to be able to say what they want without being hurried to a premature end. However, if you only have five minutes, tell them in advance.

Tip No 4: Ask for explanation of obtuse connections
Discover their logic before you decide there is no logic

If an Aspie is in full flow, it can be tempting to let them go on talking without trying to really understand what they are on about. I often find that there is in fact a connection which I had lost. A simple enquiry moves on from a patronising and passive easy listening situation to one of actual conversation where I am making an effort to understand what the other person is saying.

Tip No 5: Create rapport
Do what they are doing—let them lead, and follow so they can feel comfortable

When in doubt, when nothing seems to work, stop trying and just spend your energy creating rapport—there is power in relinquishing control because it implies acceptance and connection in a way that competitive conversation sometimes fails to do. Relax your expectations and join them in their experience. The best way into this is to bring your breathing to their level whilst finding the right distance from which to mirror their posture and movements.

Tip No 6: Check that they are understanding
*It is always good to check and go over what has been said—
never assume*

If you feel that the conversation is going out of control and the other person is drifting away, it is probably better to check that they are following so that you can backtrack and pick the subject matter up at a point of mutual understanding. This requires that you ask the person to give you a brief summary of what you have been discussing so you can hear that she or he has got hold of what is being said.

Tip No 7: Plan ahead and share the plans to allow for routines
*They may well be able to tell you what they find hard, and you
may well be able to make an escape or avoidance plan*

Many people with Asperger's are not great planners. Others sometimes make plans which overlook snags. Many difficult situations can't be avoided, but a full description of what will happen is helpful. Difficult situations can be sandwiched between reassuring routines. An agreed plan is a helpful tool.

Tip No 8: Prevent bullying at all costs
*Bullying happens, and it damages people for the rest of their
lives—do whatever it takes to prevent it from happening rather
than trying to patch things up after the event*

Bullying (the act of intimidating a weaker person to make them do something) often happens in secondary school, though it can be in the neighbourhood or at work, or indeed in the family. It can destroy the already fragile sense of self that allows us all to make decisions and move forward in our lives. Whilst it can be hard to prevent, any action taken in trying to prevent it is better than trying to adapt. It can have long-term consequences, affecting a person's self-esteem appallingly badly.

Tip No 9: Empathy
Imagine what it would be like to stand in their shoes for a
moment, with their fears and frustrations; let yourself feel it

Empathy is an identification with and understanding of another's situation, feelings and motives. People with Asperger's can find it difficult to get into, and yet sometimes they need no more than empathy to make a difference to how they feel. The search for connectedness is over when you are with a person who empathises with you. Ask yourself how life would be different for you if you were experiencing what the other person is going through.

Tip No 10: Seek continuous knowledgeable support
Everyone has a contribution to make, and the bit you do not
want to hear may be the most useful

Sometimes explanations are helpful. Doctors, psychologists, psychiatrists, teachers, Asperger experts of one form or another, sometimes other parents or other people with Asperger's: all can offer information. Anyone you feel good with can offer support, of course, although support which comes with maximum empathy and minimum advice is probably best.

Tip No 11: Claim what you want to the point of unreasonableness: do not accept No
Whether with the person who has Asperger's or with
professionals or with your partner, you have a right to be heard
and understood, and those who shout loudest usually get more
of what they want

Sometimes it takes a while to sink in. Assertiveness tells us that a good formula is: "When you do . . . I feel . . . I wish you would do . . . instead so I can feel . . ." Asking for what you want is a fundamentally good thing, and negotiating is also good, though bear in mind that the outcome of a good negotiation is that both parties are equally satisfied. Many family members end up living with circumstances which are unacceptable to them; the resultant stress is damaging to healthy life and to health. There is a process in which you give an inch in the hope that the difficulty will pass for some reason; however, it is possible that this will be accepted as the new status quo, and slowly you can be ground down. Much better to resist strongly and early, before the difficulties become entrenched.

Victory belongs to the most persevering. [Napoleon]

Tip No 12: Intervene early when things go wrong
Draw the line as soon as you feel uncomfortable

It is always better to intervene than to let things slide. If you are going to do something, then it is better to start early, before habits start to set.

Tip No 13: Look for change and development
Notice the changes and differences

It can be easy to focus on the frustrations and disappointments. Sometimes this can lead you to overlook the early signs of spring— you overlook the small signs of change. Of course, too much attention and praise can work like over-watering and drown the good intention, but remember to watch for change. Any change is a possibility.

Tip No 14: Respect
Listen and let it sink in before you make suggestions or
judgements—it is the other person who has to live his life

The first thought in coaching a person with Asperger's is that we should treat him with the same respect and assumptions that we use in coaching anyone else. It may not seem profound, but this thought combats the frustration arising from the experiences a person has had. Irrational fears, compulsive thoughts and long tortuous phrasing of complicated thoughts can lead to the person feeling that he is not listened to, for instance, and to give a person good quality, non-judgemental attention can be a powerful starting place for a coaching relationship.

Tip No 15: Work with the system
Diet? Sleep? Digestion? Medication? Relationships?
Environment?

What you see is not what you get: Asperger's is displayed in behaviour, but it is actually a systemic developmental disorder affecting the person on a number of levels. The word "system" is used here to suggest that there is an interaction and interdependence within the person, and that work to create change in one area may well affect other areas. You can, for instance, work in a behavioural style to eradicate one piece of behaviour, and you are very likely to find that another equally difficult-to-live-with piece of behaviour emerges.

Try to work on the fundamentals in order to create external change: for instance, if you seek to create trust, you may find that as the person comes to trust you, he relaxes and relates his experience more precisely, or his level of fear diminishes. Then you can work more easily on behaviour or skills acquisition. Work with the person knowing that your work will reverberate positively through the whole system of perception, thinking, beliefs and behaviour.

Tip No 16: Create powerful resource states
Do what you can to help the person feel good now

It is possible to work directly on the peptide system: meditation, for instance, creates different brain wave patterns which will direct and control a range of calming peptides in the blood. It is possible to train rats to secrete adrenaline and dogs to salivate, both to an auditory stimulus. By attaching a trusting feeling to a welcome and a handshake with me, I am sure that I am affecting this system in the person I am working with. By entering a room and taking unwelcome control of a situation I can create fear and resentment, which will be experienced as peptides in the blood. They are easier to produce than to get rid of, though, so be gentle.

Tip No 17: Future pacing
Talk though the future in the present tense and pay attention to
the response

You can change a belief by suggestion: "future pacing" is very non-threatening (you talk through future possibilities in a way that the person can accept). Will was in his flat and felt unable to go out because of his fear of others looking at him. I tried talking him through the sights and feelings he would experience in walking to the main street, and he indicated his discomfort when I asked him to imagine touching his gate and turning left into the street. He also said he would love to go to a pub. I asked him if he ever would go to a pub, and he said "Oh yes". I asked when, and he said it would take him about eighteen months. For eighteen months I was able to say: "One day, when you feel like it, you will go into a pub and we'll probably meet there", which was something he could agree with. Eighteen months later he started going to pubs again.

Tip No 18: Challenging negative generalisations
Reframe towards possibility

Challenge an unhelpful generalisation (e.g. "Women do all the housework") with information ("I always wash and iron my clothes") or questions such as "How do you know?" or "What, always?" which lead to discovering contradictions and refining of concepts.

Tip No 19: Challenging negative deletions
Reframe towards possibility

Challenge an unhelpful deletion ("I never cook") with exploratory questions such as "What can you cook?" or "How would you scramble eggs?"

Tip No 20: Challenging negative distortions
Reframe towards possibility

Challenge an unhelpful distortion (e.g. "Young men are aggressive" or "I'm always fed up when we go out" or " Women will never like me") with a contradictory example, or a question such as "How do you do that?" or "How do you know that?"

Tip No 21: Acceptance
Let him be for a while!

The obvious coaching tip is to treat each person as they truly are: a lot of coaching work is entirely about understanding how the other person operates. In this scenario, it will not matter if the person has Asperger's or is a managing director (or both!). Each person, even within the mini-spectrum of Asperger's syndrome, will be different in their perceptions, sensory awareness, thoughts, beliefs, attitudes, and so on, and each will need to be understood and accepted before they will accept coaching. However, there are patterns, which are very much the subject of this book, and recognising these patterns will help the coach.

Tip No 22: Uptime/downtime
Lead him to a better place

By talking slowly, with a very relaxed tone (though pacing the other person, not forgetting rapport), and by using gentle downward body language, as you might with a frightened horse, you can bring the subject (or a group) down to a quieter level, at which time they will be more open to listening and adjusting their behaviour. You can suggest what adjustments they might like to make. By doing the reverse, you can rev them up a bit and provoke action.

Tip No 23: Meditation
The single most important thing for you and the other person to learn

Regular meditation is a key to peaceful acceptance and physical health, and is well worth learning and teaching. If it is not possible to undertake a formal meditation session, it may be possible to sit quietly together or alone in downtime. The key to finding the value of meditation is to persist and not to expect complicated spiritual revelations, just sit.

Tip No 24: Relaxation
When you feel you are about to lose control . . .

Relaxation can be learnt: by adjusting your breathing and posture and sending your attention to each part of your body, you can find surprisingly strong areas of tension which you can release and relax quite easily. It is a technique well worth learning, as it reduces stress and increases wellbeing.

Tip No 25: Extra clarity from body language
Make your meaning clear

If the subject is not listening, you can emphasise what you are saying by using your body language to direct different thoughts to different positions around you—this helps the listener. You can also increase emphasis by gesture, of course, and with pauses in your speech.

Tip No 26: Congruence
If you believe you can, you are probably right

You have the experience of congruence when all parts of you are in agreement; the reverse is "being in two minds". It may be useful to suggest to someone that they contrast how a new thought compares with an old one they hold dear—the difference between them measures their doubtfulness.

Tip No 27: More acceptance
Give them good attention

Sometimes people become used to not being accepted. This can be because they go on too much about their own interests, or because they adopt a pattern of bullying, or because they have topics they talk about that shock, or because others around them just don't understand them too well. Although it may seem, from a NT point of view, that acceptance isn't a good position to take, from an Aspie point of view, I know very well that non-acceptance of one form or another is a common daily occurrence. Imagine how you might clam up if you knew what you were going to say was about to fall on deaf ears again. In order to move to a more relaxed place in a conversation, you may need to make your acceptance of the person explicitly clear, though you may want to separate that from what she or he is actually saying.

- Listen
- Nod, indicate acceptance (not rejection—open hands, moving in rather than away, signs of rapport)
- Repeat back what was said
- Use language like "I understand . . . I know . . . yes, and . . ."
- Avoid paraphrasing—use identical language

- If it is hard work, emphasise your acceptance language ("I know . . . I realise . . . yes, I understand . . .")
- Name their feelings and check: "You look really pissed off— is that right?" "You must be very upset about that—are you?"
- Give them a chance to notice your acceptance; watch for signs of acquiescence before you move the conversation on
- Return to what was said during the conversation

Tip No 28: Create "feelgood"
Remember when we used to . . .

By taking a person through some old and well-enjoyed experiences you can bring them to a new feeling. Alternatively, you might want to change the context by talking a walk, or making a cup of tea. If you want to change the mood, change the focus of experience.

Tip No 29: Freedom of choice
Just to remind you that you can do what you want in fact

Many people with Asperger's have had a history of other people telling them what to do. Some are themselves quite passive and used to taking the line of least resistance. Sometimes questions of authority are raised: there may be questions about the legality of certain actions, or moral imperatives to action, or it may just be that the person being coached feels weaker than you.

Coaching can be frustrating because you as coach feel as though you know perfectly well what the next step should be. You should assume that the subject feels this on a level, and consequently feels as though his own freedom of action is curtailed. It creates much better possibilities, however, if you can arrive at a place where the subject will talk freely about what he is actually most likely to do, rather than the brave but futile stance of talking as though he will do what is seen to be the best course of action.

I find it very helpful to lay out all the options in an even-handed way. Of course there are consequences (see 60 below) to all courses of action, but that does not necessarily inhibit any particular choice, and it will be better to talk about choices rather than pretend they don't exist. For instance, if the person is broke, he may well try begging in the streets, which is a course of action beyond my particular pale. If he has fixated on the young woman living across the street and is about to stuff pornography though her door, it is better that he feels OK about talking to you about his plans. More prosaically, it may be that someone who "knows" he should cook is about to go home to his parents for dinner again. Everyone knows what they "should" do. It is far more helpful to talk about what they are actually about to do. No one would ever stop drinking too much or smoking if that was untrue.

- Establish rapport
- Lay out all the options as unemotionally as possible
- Stress your lack of judgement
- Watch closely for signs of stress or rejection, and explore any option that seems to be signalled as having a "hot" reaction in either direction

Tip No 30: Sensory future pacing
Create a "future memory"

Future pacing involves encouraging a person to create a "future memory" to support a plan of action: "You might notice when you feel like doing the washing up, and you can remember how good you'll feel when you are helping out like this—warm water and soap suds". The more sensory information you put in, the more likely it is that the person will recall the thought. Stress the feelings, sounds, sights and noises that will be around at the moment of success.

Tip No 31: Talking up through the logical levels
So all parts of the person get the message

If you feel you want to introduce a new way of behaving, start by recalling the logical levels and start at the environmental level. Then, once it has been proved possible, gently and slowly talk it up towards the identity level in order to strengthen it: "You bought that drink in this very quiet pub. So you can handle money, and you will probably be able to do a whole week's shopping sometime. I know that you really want to be independent and that you are the sort of bloke who is careful with money, and I can really see you managing your own money because that's the kind of bloke you really are. Isn't it?"

Tip No 32: Leading the change process
Experience what you want the person to experience

Faced with someone stuck in any of these stages, it may be helpful to focus the coaching on the present stage and associated feelings, and then to lead gently to the next stage. Acceptance and acknowledgement that the person wants the problem to go away can be followed by a lead towards anger. The best lead is to go there yourself, and in the case of anger this has to be done with subtlety and control.

Tip No 33: Parts work
When you are in two minds, you can talk to both parts of your mind separately

When someone indicates more than one point of view in their mind, ask them to speak for the disagreeing part, and ask what that part wants. Sometimes it is useful to give it a personality; sometimes it is enough just to articulate the point of view and let it be heard. When it is clear what the disagreeing part wants, find a way to understand how that aim can be achieved through the new behaviour. "Not sure about this washing up thing." "What might be against it?" "Don't want to have to do it every night 'cause that wouldn't be fair." "Well, if it's fairness you want . . . what would make it fair?" "Maybe just weekdays?" "And what could be fair at weekends—perhaps you could clear the table instead?"

Tip No 34: Position change
Get up and move about

If the discussion is about another person's point of view, go to downtime and ask them to move to the second person's position, have a look at the first person, and find out what it is like to be in that position.

Tip No 35: Time frames
Be clear about the time frames and help the person move into the mid term

Short term is reactive: you do what you have to do or what you always do. Long term is when you have got to where you want to be. Middle term is tricky as it involves doing new things in order to make the passage from short term to long term. It is very helpful to change time frames to enable people to imagine changing their behaviour without being too frightened.

Tip No 36: Time lines
Let them explore the future by moving through it

Most people structure their time either from left to right or from rear to front. Whichever it is, ask them to point to their next birthday. Lay out an imaginary line from now to then, and ask them to walk along it while you talk them though some of the milestones of change and find out what comes to their mind.

Tip No 37: Reassurance
Let the unconscious mind attach the required meaning

Using "artfully vague" language you can suggest (in downtime language) that s/he knows exactly what to do and will remember all s/he needs to know at the right time. "Oh, I know you'll know what to do when you get there . . . you don't have to know now, but you won't let yourself get into real trouble anyway, will you? When the time comes, you'll know . . ."

Tip No 38: Find the cause—TDS
Just ask and listen!

The unconscious mind knows a lot more than it lets on. Ask (in downtime): "When did you first feel this feeling?" and accompany yourself with a swishing sound to give a signal that something different is required. Wait. See what happens and explore how that relates back to childhood experience.

Tip No 39: Repetition
Three times at least!

As a trainer I learnt that you need to say everything three times in order to be heard. Say important things several times in different ways if you want them to be remembered.

Tip No 40: Failure as feedback
Keep the door open—learn from everything

This is a reframing exercise, and with Aspies it needs to be stressed (said three times). Failure is a perception, not a fact. A plan which does not deliver the expected and desired result is food for learning: was it the plan, the execution of the plan, the circumstances? Why did it not work? If you can inculcate this framework in the person's head, then the next question is: "What do you need to change for next time?"

Tip No 41: Reframing
Look at it another way—a better way

A frame is the set of beliefs which leads you to experience an occurrence in a particular way: "I never talk to anyone at parties." "Young men are aggressive." Meet "I never go to parties because I never talk to anyone" with "Well, what do you need to do to make this one different?" and "I never go to the bus station because there are gangs of aggressive youths there" with "When did you last get beaten up or threatened? Well, you're older now, out of the age range for street violence".

Tip No 42: Well formed outcome
Clear and controllable, worthwhile and believable

This is fully explained above: the nine step answer includes:

- A positive description of what you do want
- The evidence you will see, hear and feel
- Is it in your control? What do you have to do to put action in your control?
- What do you lose by doing or getting this, and how can you continue to get it in some other way?
- With whom, when and where do you want this?
- Is it worth the effort?
- The time?
- The money?
- Do you believe you can have this?

Tip No 43: Outcome framing
"So what would it be like if . . . ?"

Turn any problem into a possibility by asking the person to consider what he or she wants to happen. Problems lead to a full stop, but a question such as "what do you want to happen?" leads to planning and hence action.

Tip No 44: Separate feelings from thoughts
Separate fact from fiction

Feelings are true but individual thoughts are opinions: interesting but not true. Facts are facts and are true. It can be very helpful to separate the three categories, especially in times of conflict.

Tip No 45: What do you want?
Back to basics

The full well formed outcome model is sometimes too much, though you can keep it in your head. When in doubt, ask: "What do you want?" The answer can be in terms of feelings, situations, plans, time frames—anything. It is invariably a useful intervention.

Tip No 46: Circle of excellence
Careful preparation of a person's feelings

"Imagine a circle in front of you. This is the place in which you can perform as you want to (for a coming event). What states do you need to have access to in order to do as well as you can? When did you experience this state before? See, hear, feel that time, and as you feel it fully, step into the circle." (You then anchor them with a touch.) Out of the circle. Repeat for the next state until you have covered the whole list of desirable states.

"Stand outside the circle. Imagine this coming event, and as you enter it, step into the circle (you touch the anchor point) and feel, see, hear what it is like to do this . . ."

Tip No 47: Anchors
Create automatic recall: push the buttons

Any feeling or thought can be anchored to a sensation (as with Pavlov's dog's association). A good anchor is sensory, immediate, and accurately applied to the peak of the experience. You can formally use touch, or informally a vocal trick or a flip of a coin. When the anchor is repeated, the thought or feeling will tend to return.

Tip No 48: Connection
"I like being with you . . ."

Create a feeling of connection though establishing rapport. Add to it with anchors (shaking hands, patting shoulders, making a cup of tea, saying the same things, incense). Most importantly, avoid hurrying and controlling things for a while to establish the connection first.

Tip No 49: Including family perspectives
What do the others think?

Use position change (34) to enhance the ability to check out what another person in the family might feel about a plan. Encourage the person to consider what the other person may hold as a particular point of view and whether they may be right.

Reframe the discussion towards a planning perspective so it is easier to change plans if you want to without losing pride.

Tip No 50: Family ecology
Boundaries, consequences, negotiations, space

Who do you want to be included in this, where, and when? Answer the same questions for the other members of the family. If the subject does not know what another person in the family might say, have them pretend that they do. Does this plan suit the family, and if not, what can you do about it (if you want to)? What will be the consequences of doing this your way?

Tip No 51: Habit implantation
Learning a new habit is not easy—teamwork!

Repetition and routine will implant habits, but it will take the better part of six months before the habit is ingrained. In between times, motivation, support, a journal, and acceptance of stop-and-starting are needed.

Tip No 52: Boundaries
Establishing absolutes

Some areas are no go (my wallet, my bank account, my clothes). Consistency and absolute adherence are required to maintain boundaries under threat. Hand signals may help in explaining this (hands chopping across the body or the face, slow repletion with little body movement). Mainly it is about your willingness to continue being firm and clear.

Tip No 53: DISC profiling
Learning and personality styles

There are a small number of very obvious dynamics which separate the large group of people with Asperger's from smaller specific groups. I am currently exploring the unprecedented use of an established personality profiling tool which provides a highly functional description of "do and don't communication behaviour" as well as description of personality style. It is an online tool which can be supported with a telephone conversation.

Tip No 54: Leading by example
Be the change you want to see

If someone is going through the change cycle or if you feel that some emotion is lacking, it is good to go there yourself—acting may be good enough—in order to encourage him to make the move. So if you feel that he may have had enough of denial and anger and it is time to get on to depression, it may be good to start talking about depression.

Tip No 55: Naming feelings
Give them the words and clarity

Tell people what you think they are feeling—if you are wrong, it won't matter; they will correct you. If you are right, they may be really grateful that you told them what is going on.

Tip No 56: Modelling
How do you do that?

Enquire how your subject does something they are good at. Enquire about the sensations, thoughts, feelings and signals they use to do it. Help them see how this pattern may help them in a different task. It is also an interesting conversation in terms of unwanted behaviour: "How do you go about getting angry?"

Tip No 57: Soundbites and slogans
Tohellwivit!

Label processes or thoughts with easily remembered names. A subject may have a "tohellwivit" mechanism, for instance. Proverbs can be useful too: a problem shared is a problem halved.

Tip No 58: Congruence test
I don't know much but I know what I like!

Get him to describe exactly how he knows he believes in something. Compare this with a suggested change to help him to discover if it is something he really cares about. "You know you believe that you are male? How do you know that you know that?" "Well, I just do." "And how does that feel to you?" "Strong, obvious, unchallengeable . . ." "Where do you feel it?" "In my gut!" "So about this idea that you can live on your own now . . ."

Tip No 59: Installing thought viruses
Tell him good things about himself—give him a gift

Talk him into downtime, establish rapport, give him back his best thoughts about himself, in your view, in a way which is difficult to disagree with: "I can see you are a good man, and I know you are strong and intelligent . . . you can do anything if you have the right support." Then add a specific suggestion in a non-threatening way: "You won't take money from my wallet because you won't really want to."

Tip No 60: Consequences
If this, then that: night follows day, and the rule is the rule

Well formed consequences are fully in your control, not too distasteful to you, appropriate and fair. You may impose them or let nature take its course. "If you come home drunk, I won't let you in."

"If you hit me, I will call the police." "If you spend all your money, I won't lend you any." "If you don't do the washing up, I am not cooking for you." "If you are not down here in the kitchen by 8.30, I will pull the duvet off you." They must be applied consistently throughout the ensuing trial of boundaries until he surrenders.

Tip No 61: Time frames (short, mid, long)
You have to make a move into the mid term in order to make change happen

Short term is a reactive space in which you do what you have to. This does not produce change.

Long term is whatever you want it to be (and you make a choice by doing nothing, so long term can be just the same as today if you make no changes).

Mid term is where you make progressive strategic steps towards your chosen long-term goal. It is uncomfortable, stressy and unpredictable, but necessary.

Tip No 62: Developing family responsibility
Other points of view—how can you support the changes going on? What do you fear?

The family is the biggest influence on a person with Asperger's, and indeed on the rest of the NTs too. Therefore, the family needs to be included and ready to support any changes, and the family may also need to be encouraged and supported and coached in making changes amongst themselves. Asking the person with Asperger's to do it all himself is sometimes very close to scapegoating, in which the one individual is cast out and expected to take all the sins of the family with him.

Tip No 63: Teamwork
Working together feels good

Teamwork happens when all people agree with the task in hand and share out responsibilities, relying on each other. It is enhanced by some "feelgood" time. With an Aspie, this may have to be created, and he may have to be told what is going on more than the NTs.

Mutual feedback is part of teamwork, and the feeling is one of group rather than individual.

Tip No 64: Problem solving
Identify the problem clearly

- Agree that you want to solve it.
- Decide what to replace it with.
- Dream up as many ways as possible to solve it.
- Choose one, make a plan about how you would do this (use the well formed outcome).
- Have a sharp-nosed, critical look at it.
- Amend the plan.

Tip No 65: Saying No
Say it you mean it, mean it if you say it

Only say No if you mean it and if you can ensure that you are in control. Make sure those around you support you. Use hand signals and body posture to look fearsomely sure of yourself (chop your hands, draw yourself up to your full height, say No, be still, retain eye contact—stare him out if necessary; turn away). Do not enter into discussion. After a while, change the subject or activity. Use sparingly.

Tip No 66: Specific coaching
Teaching tips

To help someone learn a new skill or piece of behaviour, break it down into tiny steps, create procedures, and practise and demonstrate each step. Because most difficult things have choices, create a flow chart or a mind map to enable the person to follow the choices. Use repetition of each step to help establish skills and familiarity, then link the steps together.

Tip No 67: Opening doors
Problem planning: what if . . . ?

Talk through a situation, identifying all the choices available, opening the door to each possibility and rejecting or accepting it as you talk.

This creates a really strong mental rehearsal which seems to help people who use that mental strategy, and of course you can drop a few helpful suggestions in as you go: "So when you go for this job interview, you might be nervous, so you might wake up really early, but you don't want to do that—stay in bed till it's time to get up. Leave enough time, though, so you can have a shower and feel good, and choose your best interview clothes. I don't know if you'll want breakfast, but you'll know when you get there—especially if you leave enough time. Maybe just some coffee and a bit of toast—you wouldn't want a big greasy spoon thing. And you know the journey; though it might be raining, so you may have to take your umbrella . . ." And so on.

Tip No 68: Metaphors
It's like a . . . and I can tell you why!

These are either very helpful or dead as a dodo with some Aspies. Some people just don't make sense of them; others love them. I heard of someone who decided to conduct himself at work like Superman and changed his behaviour for the better immediately, for instance.

Annie talked about Asperger's as being like living behind a translucent brick wall with a few bricks missing—a strong and detailed representation of a complex experience.

Metaphors can carry a lot of information in this way, but they have to come naturally, and forcing them doesn't work. You may be able to ask someone what it is like to be shy, for instance, and if you keep on asking, you may get to a metaphor which has more to it than the usual conversation.

Tip No 69: Being artfully vague: Milton model
When you notice how you are relaxing right now . . . when you
feel good with me in our safe space . . . when you feel like that . . .

By deleting content, distorting connections and generalising, you can create things to say which cannot be disagreed with and will occupy the conscious mind, so you can have greater access to the unconscious—good for creating thought viruses, good for talking people into downtime. You need to use your tone of voice in a gentle way to create downtime mood as you do this:

"As you sit there, you can image how easy it is to relax. Everyone relaxes, and you can relax right now."

"I can see you are a good man, because I know one when I meet one, and you are a good man."

Tip No 70: Creating "feelgood"
Lean on me /

Create rapport as strongly as you can. Concentrate on the experience you are sharing with the subject. Use "we" and "us", and gentle physical contact if that is possible. Avoid things that make him uncomfortable (idiosyncratic things like eye contact—you will know). Move yourself into a "feelgood" state: focus on the successes you are having and the sensory experiences, choose to enjoy yourself. Make him the most important person around for a while.

Tip No 71: Building recall
What did you see, hear, feel, smell, taste . . . ?

All these tips are about creating multi-sensory associations: you can make them up, but here are some suggestions:

- Suggest he will manage to remember this remarkably well—ask him to remember to notice how well he does recall when the time comes.
- Lay out the thing you want him to remember in steps or stages. Not more than five, though each can have sub-steps.
- Use actual things or a picture or a numbered list for him to see.
- Make sure you repeat it at least three times.
- Use sounds or touch as "anchors" that he can associate (fingers are also good as anchors and markers).
- Give him pictures to associate. (Mrs Bird: squawking on the tree: Go to the fence post office, get stamps there. STAMP!)
- Get him to say it with some movements (fingers in the air, one step forward for each thing to be remembered).
- Suggest that he will remember just what you have said, that it will all come back to him just when he needs it. Remind him to notice how well he does.

Tip No 72: Habits elimination
For ever!

If you want to stop wanting to eat something ever again:

- Be sure you want to stop eating this (A).
- Think of something that is disgusting to you (B).
- Imagine in a big plate of that disgusting B in front of you. Smell it, eat it in your imagination. Squeeze your thumb and little finger together as you do this. Imagine the textures, tastes and smells of eating it as you do this. Keep going till you are revolted. When you feel a bit sick, stop.
- Imagine a plate of what you are going to stop eating (A).
- Make your imagined picture of this big and bright, then bigger and brighter, then really big and really, really bright. Imagine bringing it close to you and right through you and out the other side.
- Squeeze thumb and little finger together, recall the taste of what you hate (B) while you imagine eating what you are stopping (A). Imagine the two mixed together. Continue to imagine eating the two, the smells, tastes and textures all filling you up. When you can't do any more, stop.
- Think about the food you are giving up (A) and notice how it's changed.

Tip No 73: Leading by demonstration
I am feeling . . .

If you want to open up a more emotional conversation, visit the emotions first yourself, gently. Talk about them—anger, or depression, or whatever feels right: share how you are, avoid prescribing how he might be feeling but suggest that he might be going in this direction in the future; give him some of the signs, perhaps. Avoid stealing his thunder by being overcome, and leave him lost in space to experience whatever he experiences.

Tip No 74: "Clevertalk"
Agree, find common ground, take them away from conflict

Essentially, you use carefully phrased language to seek an agreement at some level, or at least to step round an argument in order to move forward. Here are some examples:

I think you are trying to manipulate me.
It is really important to know if someone is trying to get you to do something you don't want to do. You know, I don't think this is about you being manipulated as much as about you finding a new way to do things.

You're ganging up with the doctors and social workers to get me locked up!
I'd really love to know how you think I'd do that. The only way you can get locked up is when five people all agree that you are a risk to yourself or to others: they won't even ask me!

Nobody knows the trouble I've seen—my life is so hard!
You know, I think I do. But I will never know if I'm right unless you tell me. It's a terrible thing to feel as though you're on your own.

Tip No 75: More "Clevertalk"
The same words . . .

Use the subject's exact words and ask a clean question:

I feel scared.

- And when you feel scared like that scared, what happens just before?
- Or: What's behind that scared?
- Or: What happens next?
- Or: When you feel scared like that scared that you feel right now, what happens next?

Continue in this vein and you can access some deep information.

Tip No 76: Moving beyond co-dependence
Get support and move forward

Co-dependence is a pattern that leads people into accepting and even relying on the presence of a problem. Clear factual communication and honest consequences for actions are required to help people with Asperger's syndrome to take responsibility for their own lives, and yet the families often develop in a way in which the whole family is supporting the continuing dependence of the person with Asperger's. The coaching tip is to get whatever support is needed in order to address the behaviour patterns within the whole family.

REFERENCES

Attwood, T. (2006). *The Complete Guide to Asperger's Syndrome*. London: Jessica Kingsley.

Bandler, R. & Grinder, J. (1975). *Patterns of the Hypnotic Techniques of Milton Erickson*. Capitola, CA: Meta Publications.

Bandler, R. & Grinder, J. (1975). *The Structure of Magic: A Book about Language and Therapy*. Palo Alto, CA: Science & Behavior Books.

Baron-Cohen, S. (2003). *The Essential Difference: The Truth about the Male and Female Brain*. New York: Basic Books.

Charvet, S.R. (1997). *Words That Change Minds: Mastering the Language of Influence*. Dubuque, IA: Kendall/Hunt.

Cooper, J.E. (1994). *Pocket Guide to the ICD-10 Classification of Mental and Behavioural Disorders*. Oxford: Churchill Livingstone.

Diamond, J. (1991). *The Rise and Fall of the Third Chimpanzee*. London: Vintage.

Fitzgerald, M. (2004). *Autism and Creativity: Is there a Link between Autism in Men and Exceptional Ability?* Hove: Brunner-Routledge.

Frith, U. (1991). *Autism and Asperger Syndrome*. Cambridge: Cambridge University Press.

Fromm, E. (1956). *The Art of Loving*. London: Harper Perennial, 2000.

Gallwey, T. (1974). *The Inner Game of Tennis: The Classic Guide to the Mental Side of Peak Performance*. London: Pan, 1986.

Grandin, T. & Scariano, M. (1986). *Emergence: Labeled Autistic*. New York: Warner.

Jackson, L. (2002). *Freaks, Geeks and Asperger Syndrome: A User Guide to Adolescence*. London: Jessica Kingsley.

Lawson, W. (2000). *Life Behind Glass: A Personal Account of Autism Spectrum Disorder*. London: Jessica Kingsley.

Maslow, A. (1943). A Theory of Human Motivation. *Psychological Review* 50: 370–396.

O'Connor, J. & McDermott, I. (1996). *Principles of NLP*. London: HarperCollins.

Pert, C. (1997). *Molecules of Emotion*. New York: Simon & Schuster.

Rogers, C. (1961). *On Becoming a Person: A Therapist's View of Psychotherapy*. London: Constable.

Sacks, O. (1995). *An Anthopologist on Mars: Seven Paradoxical Tales*. London: Picador.

Sainsbury, C. (2000). *Martian in the Playground: Understanding the Schoolchild with Asperger's Syndrome*. London: Lucky Duck.

Snyder, C.R. & Lopez, S.J. (2001). *Handbook of Positive Psychology*. Oxford: Oxford University Press.

Wildman, D.E., Uddin, M., Liu, G., Grossman, L.I. & Goodman, M. (2003). Implications of natural selection in shaping 99.4% nonsynonymous DNA identity between humans and chimpanzees: enlarging genus Homo. *Proc. Nat. Acad. Sci. USA* 100: 7181–8.

Willey, L.H. (1999). *Pretending to be Normal: Living with Asperger's Syndrome*. London: Jessica Kingsley.

Williams, D. (1996). *Autism: An Inside-Out Approach: An Innovative Look at the Mechanics of Autism and its Developmental Cousins*. London: Jessica Kingsley.

LINKS AND SITES

Jane Meyerding: http://mjane.zolaweb.com/
Robyn Steward: http://www.robynsteward.com/
Paul Shattock: http://osiris.sunderland.ac.uk/autism/
National Autistic Society: http://www.nas.org.uk/
Brookdale Care: http://www.brookdalecare.co.uk/
The Priory: http://www.priorygroup.com/
Hesley Group: http://www.thehesleygroup.com/
DSM IV: http://mysite.verizon.net/res7oqx1/index.html
Bill Goodyear: http://www.billgoodyear.org

INDEX